Coloring book for adults and kids beautiful cupcake image for design

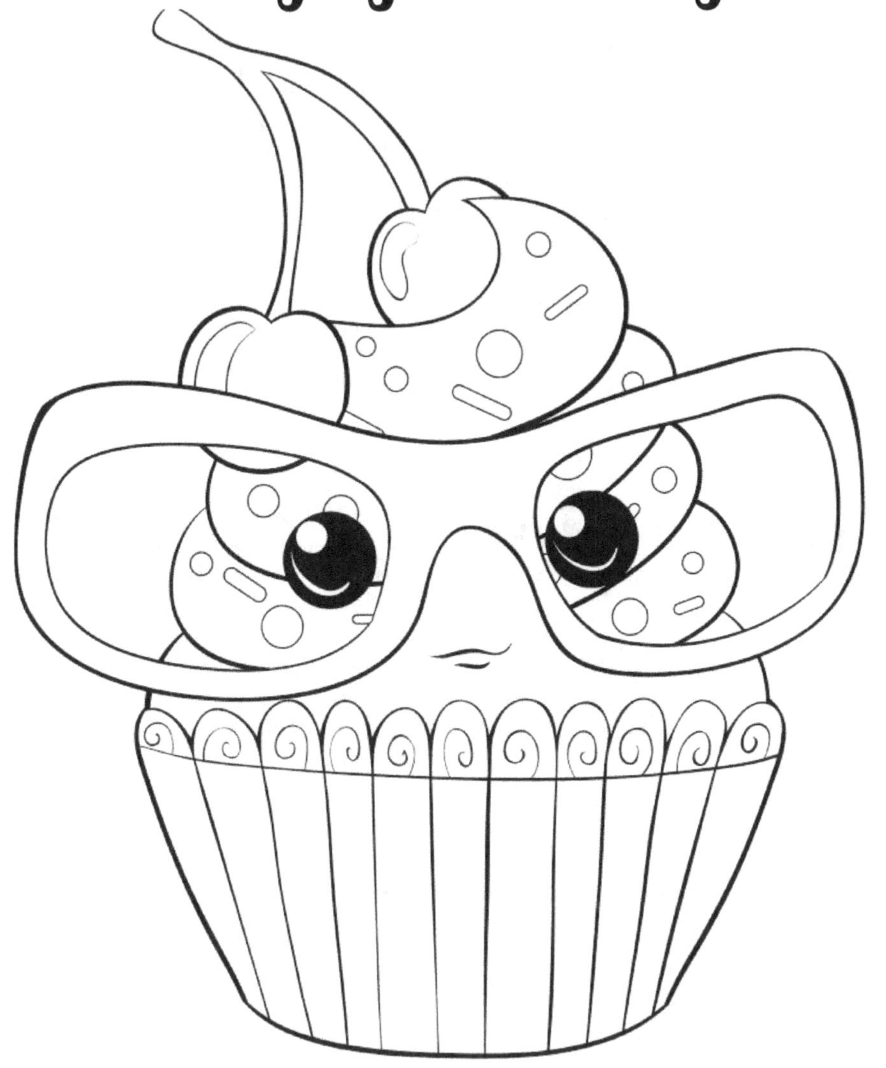

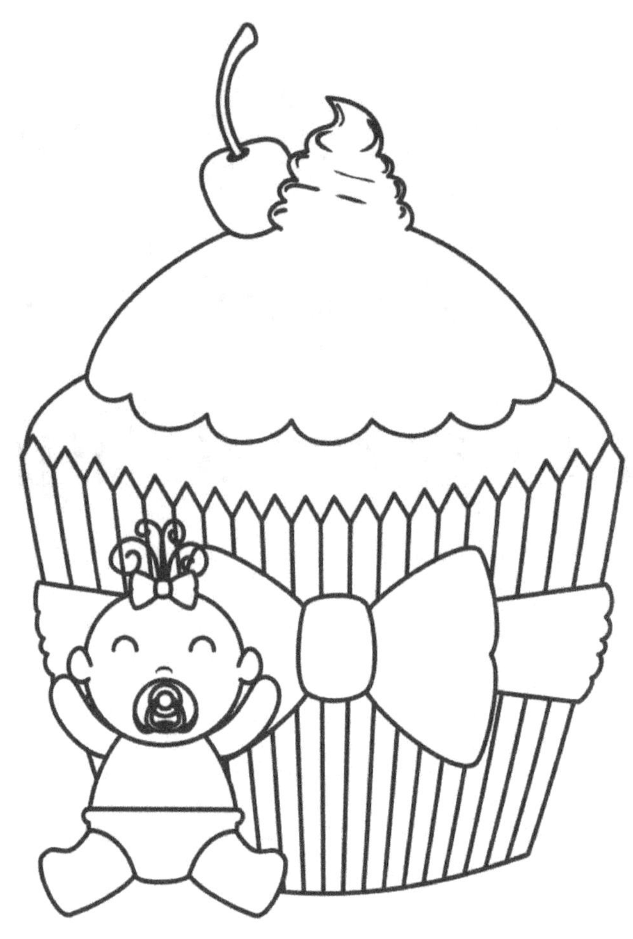

This coloring book is
belongs to

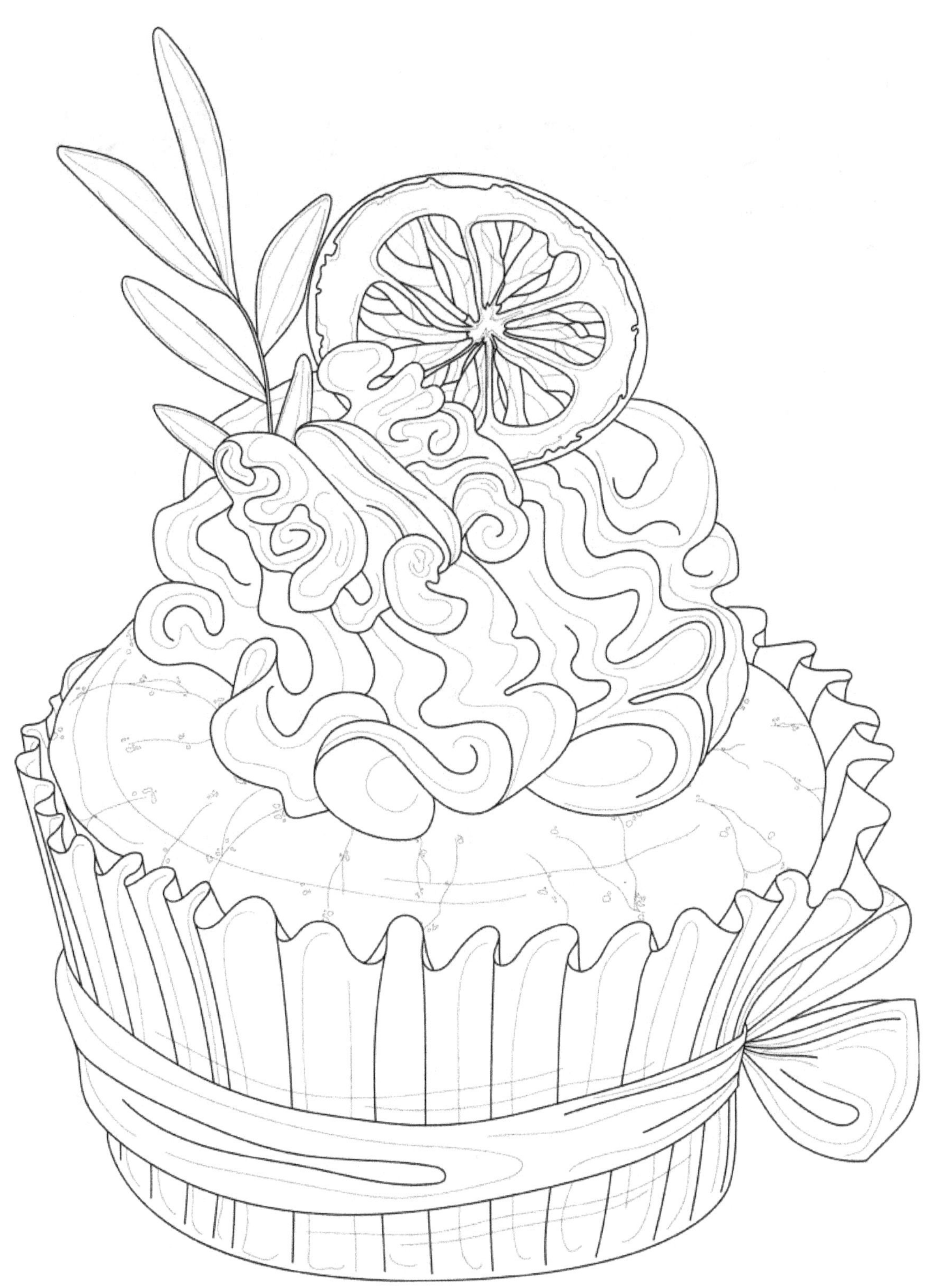

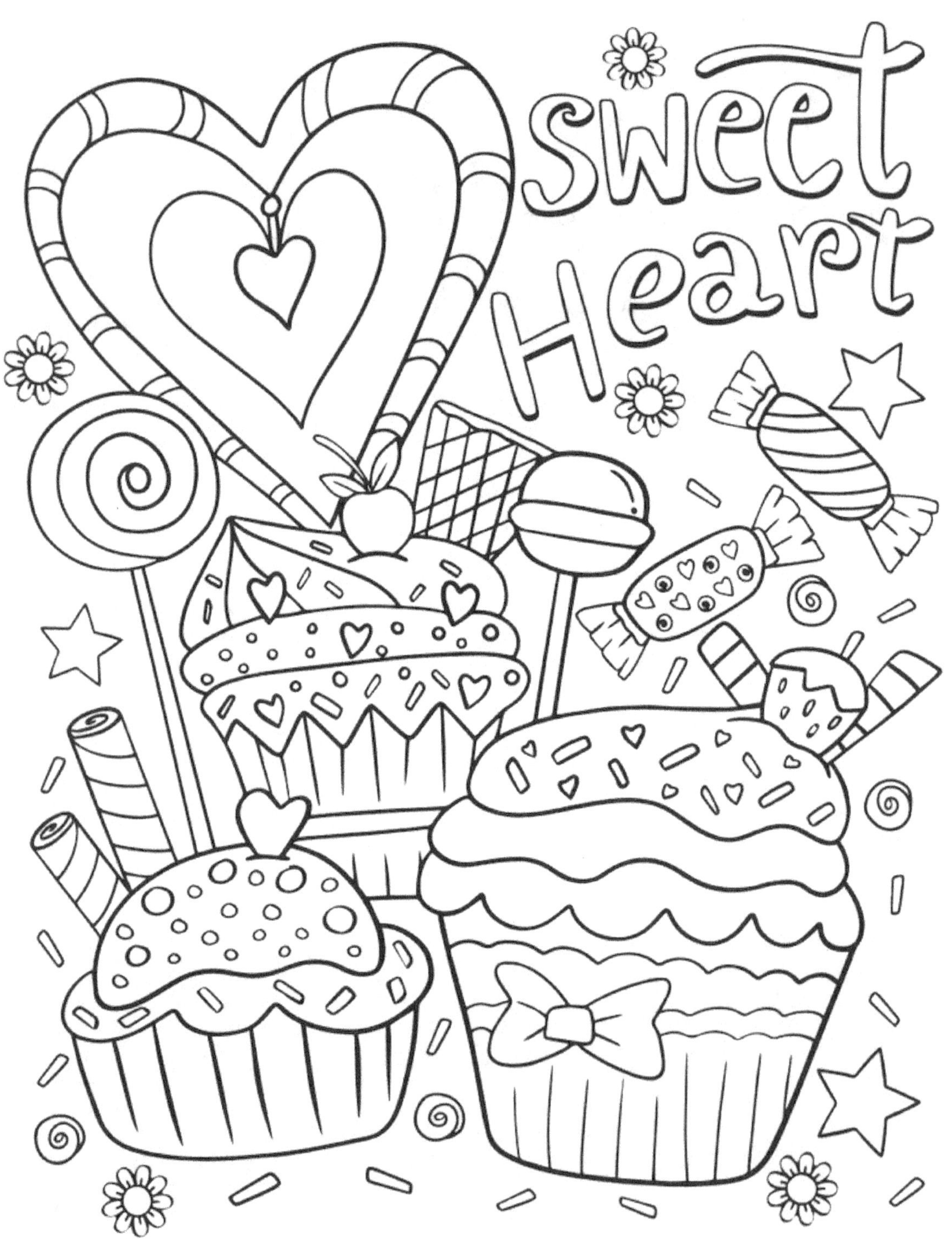

sweet
Heart

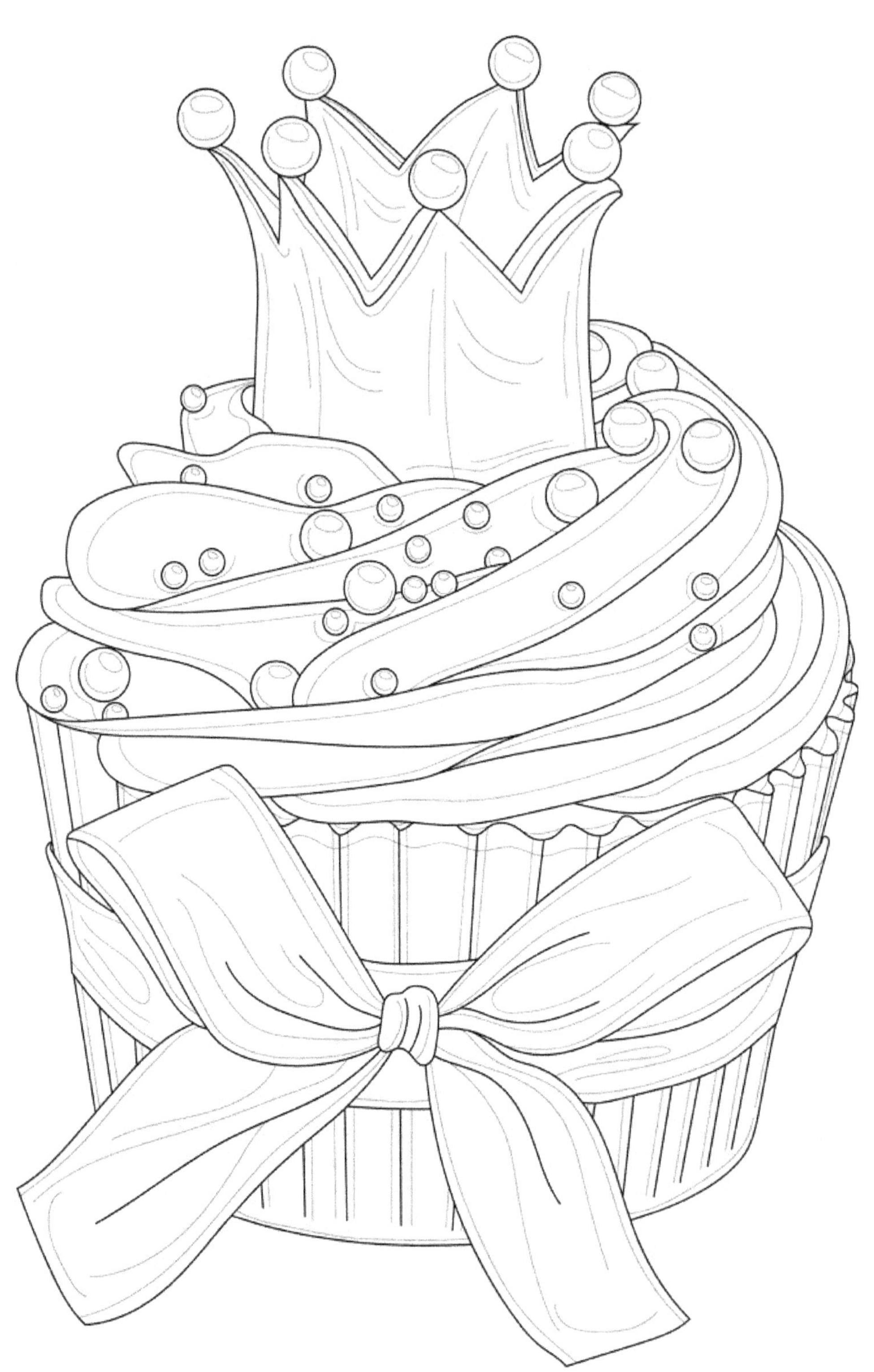

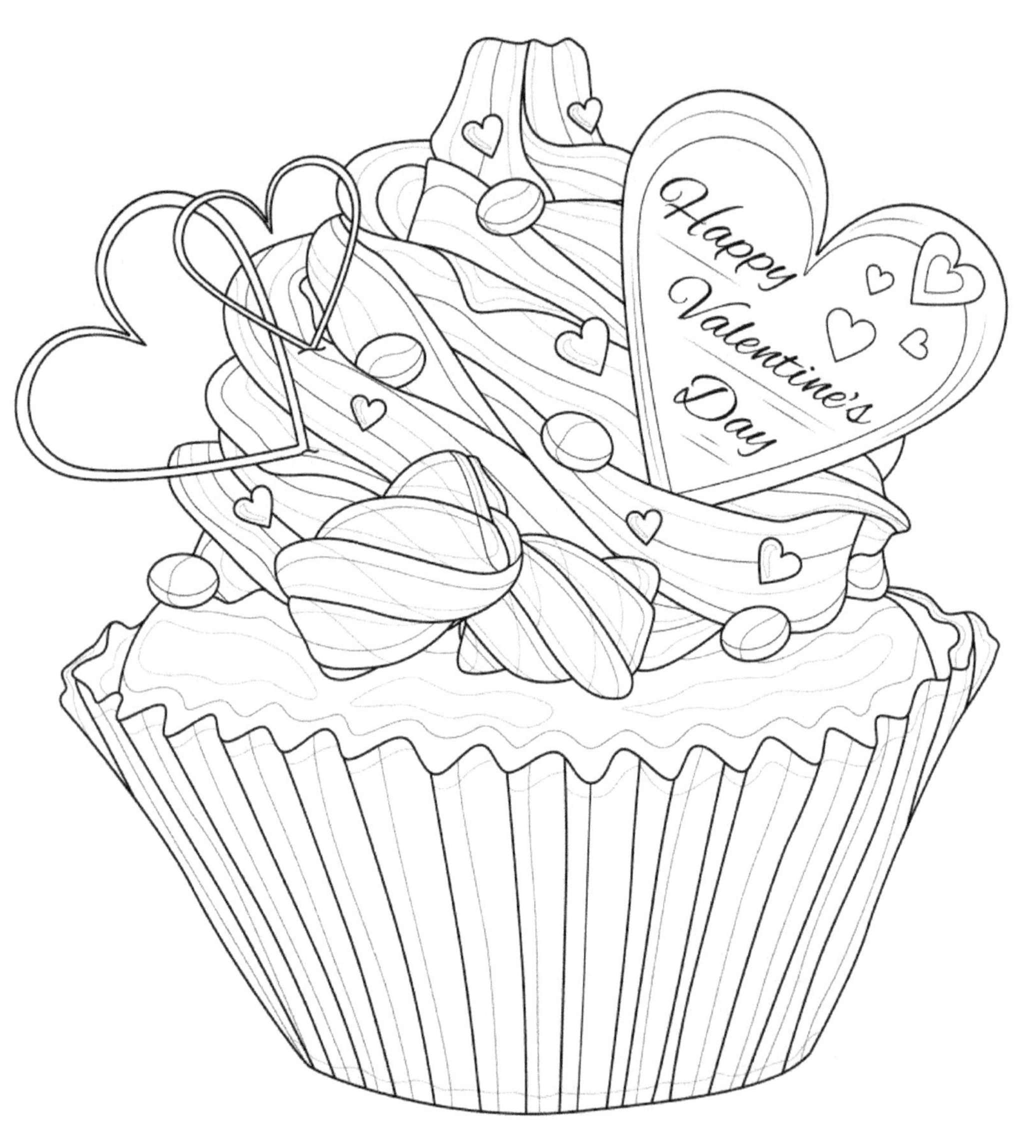
Happy
Valentine's
Day

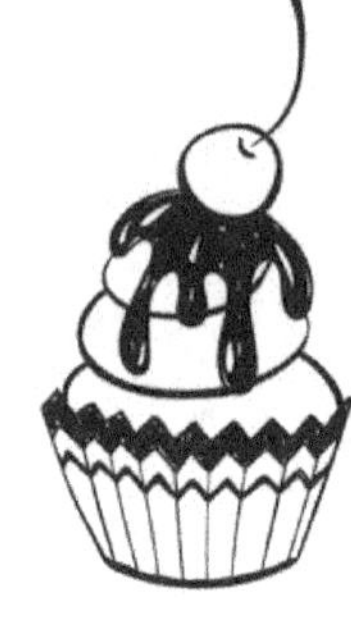
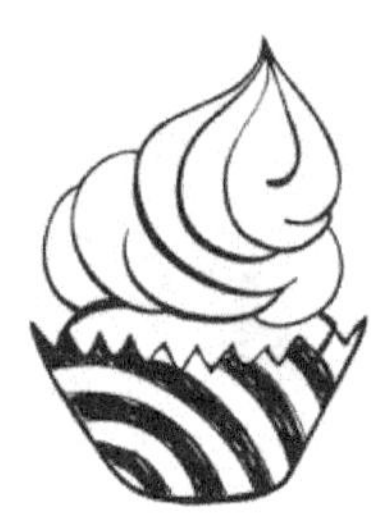
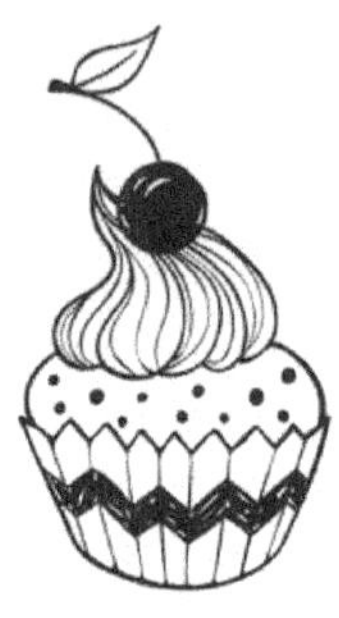
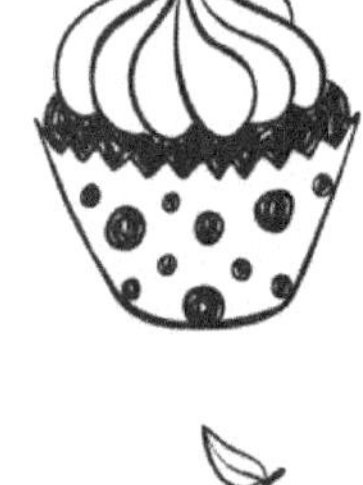
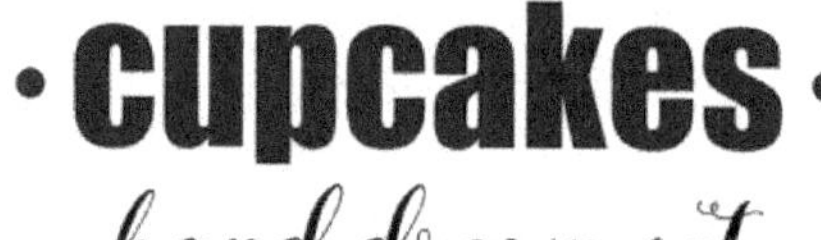

· cupcakes ·
hand drawn set

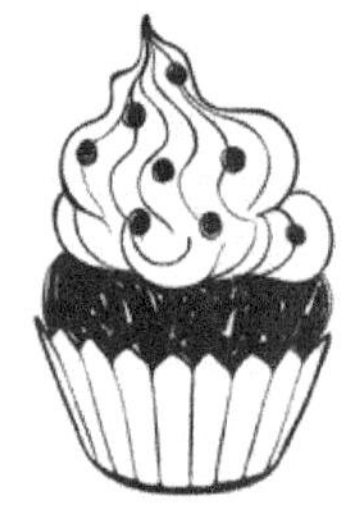
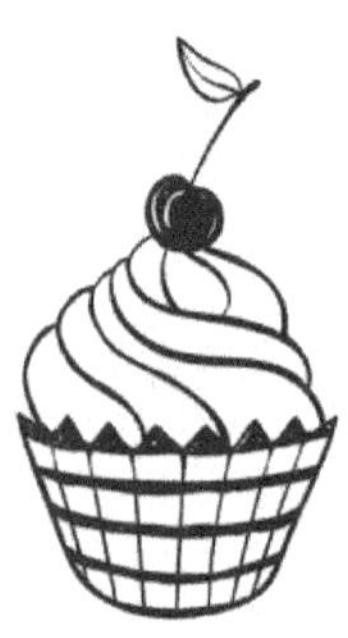
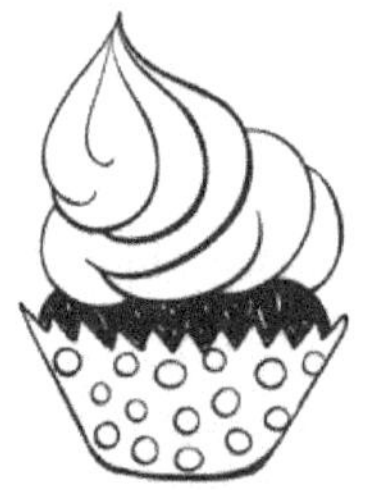
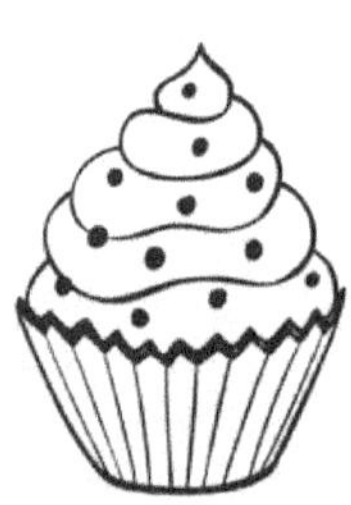
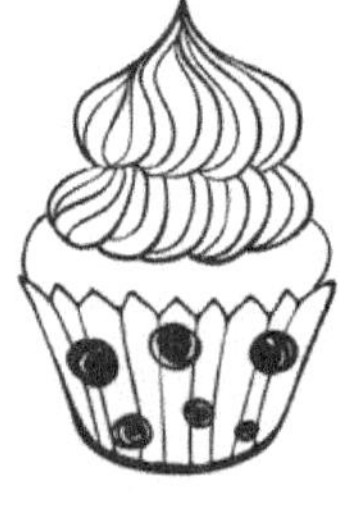

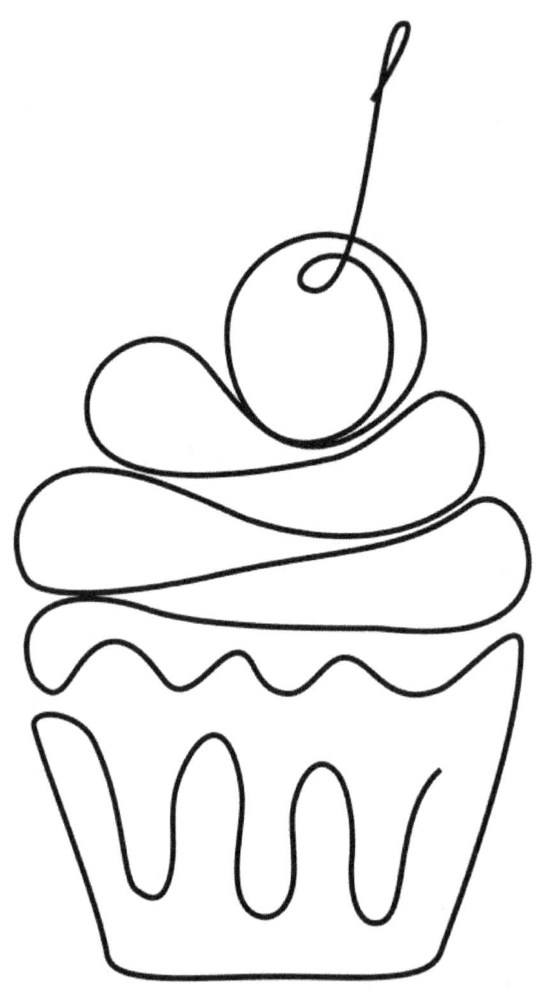

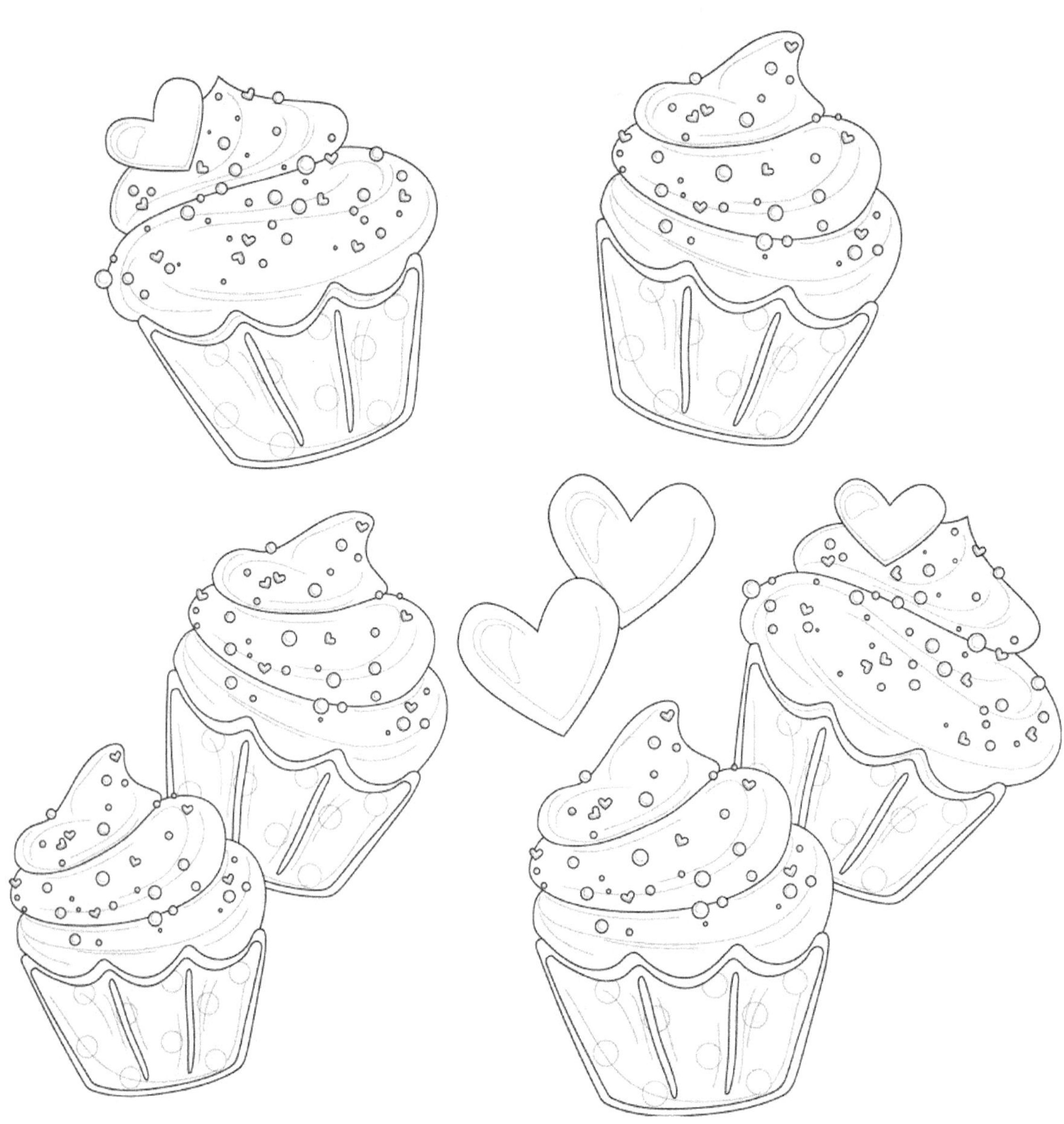

cake

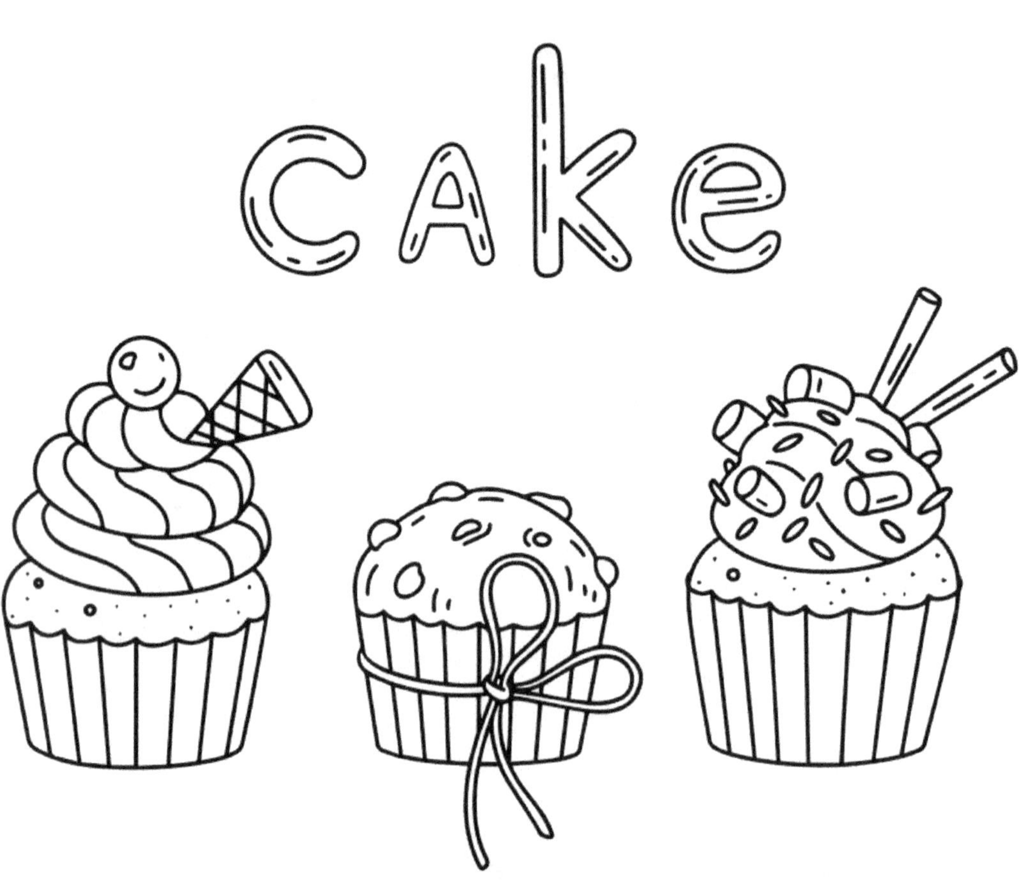

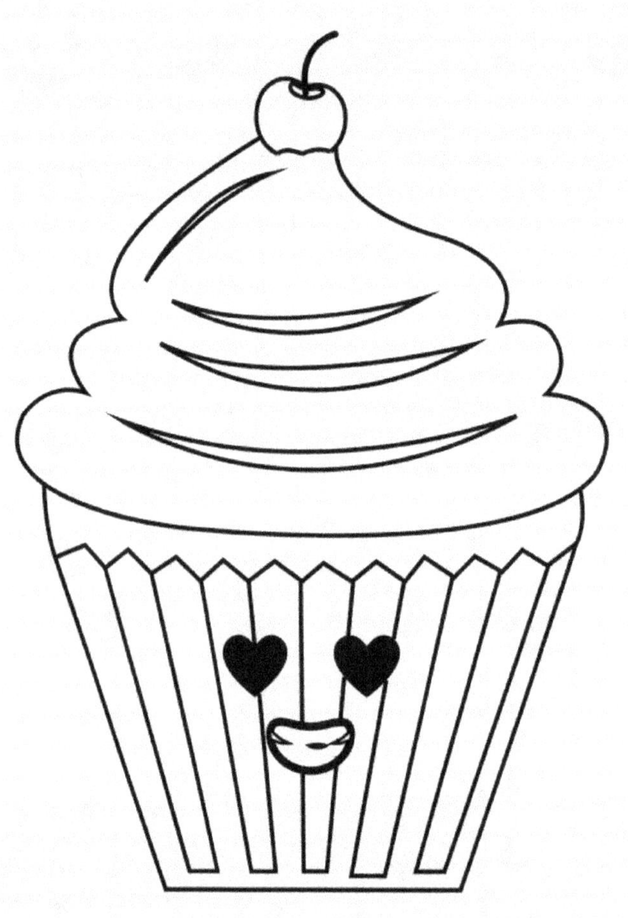

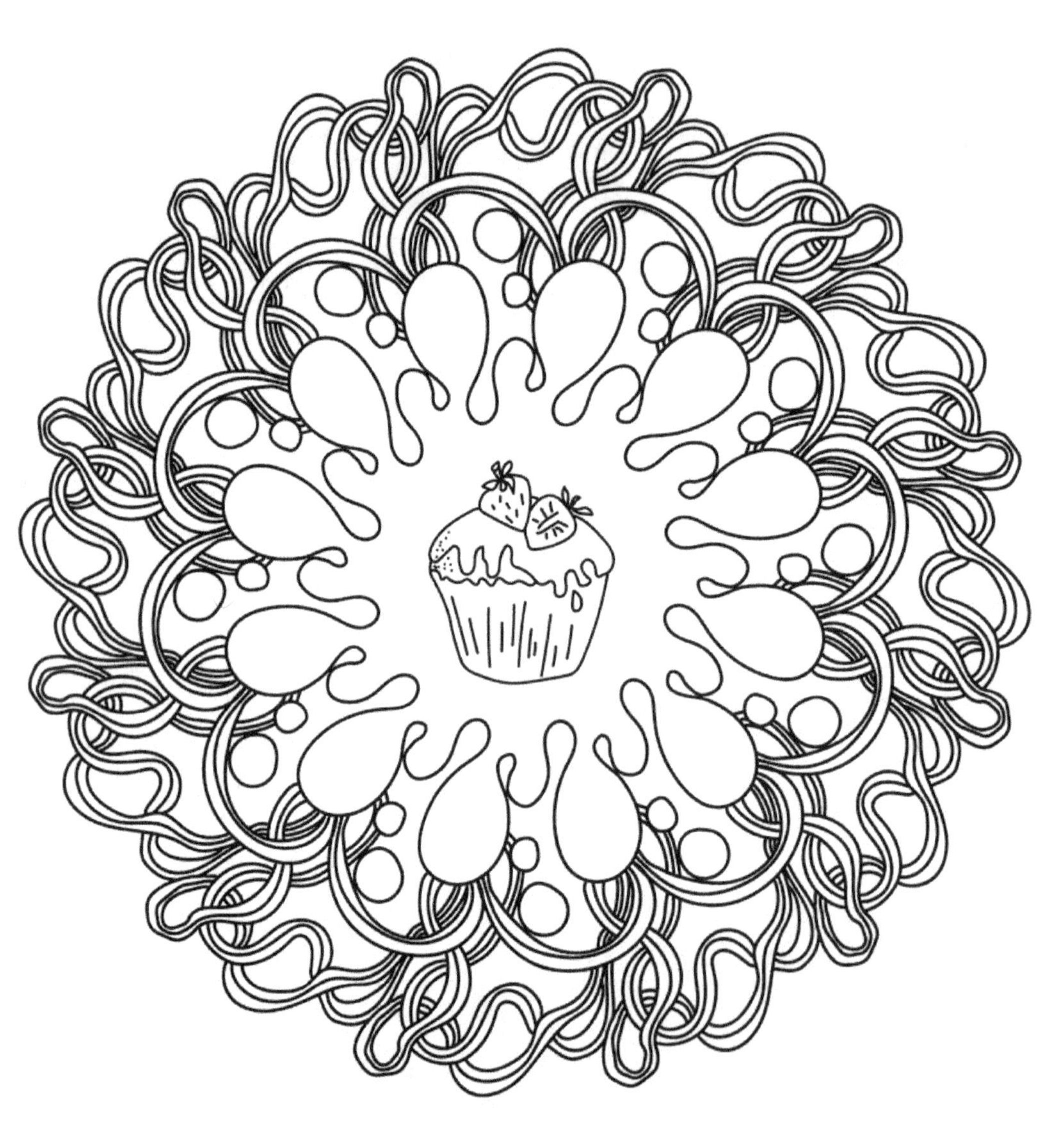

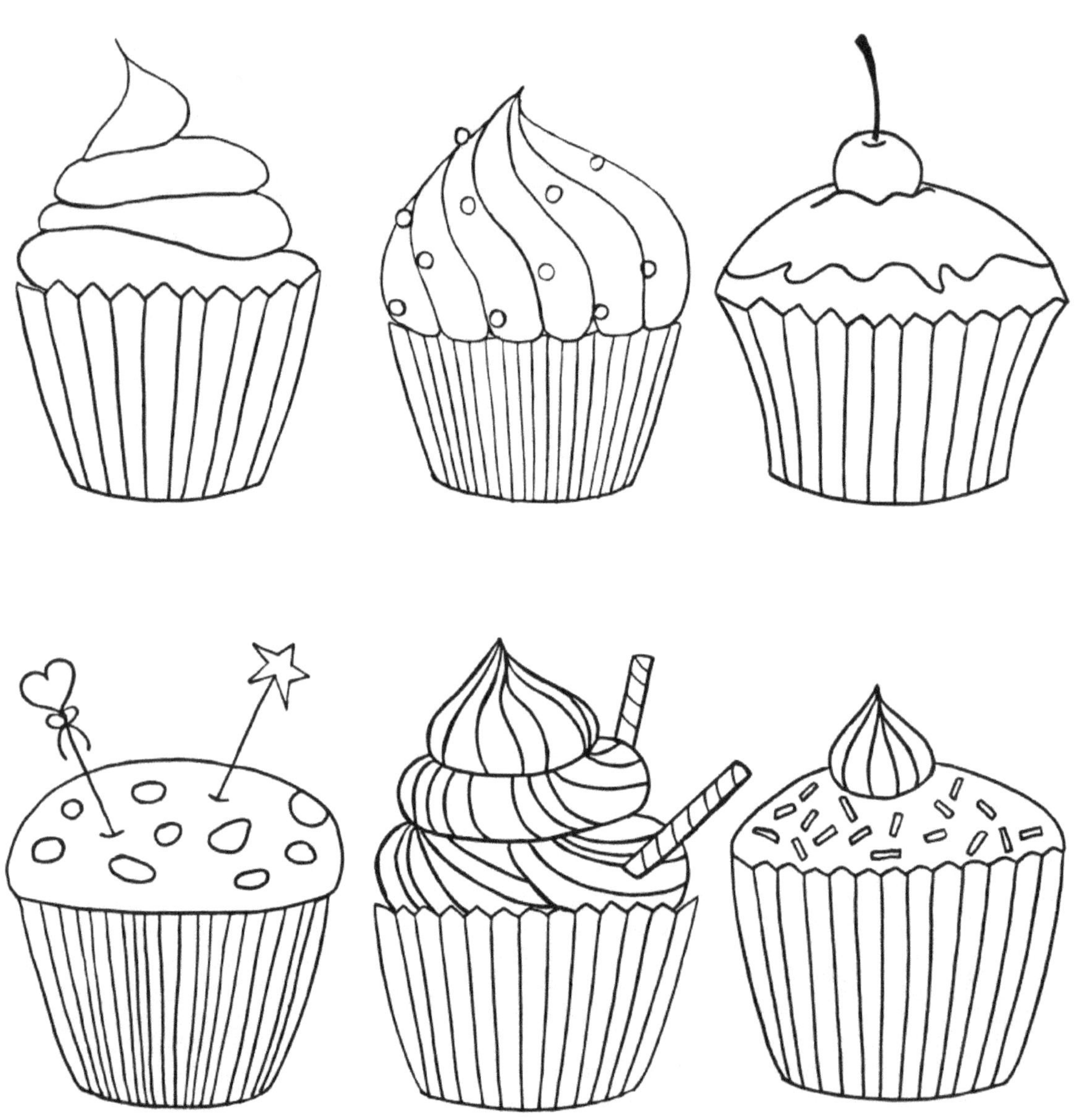

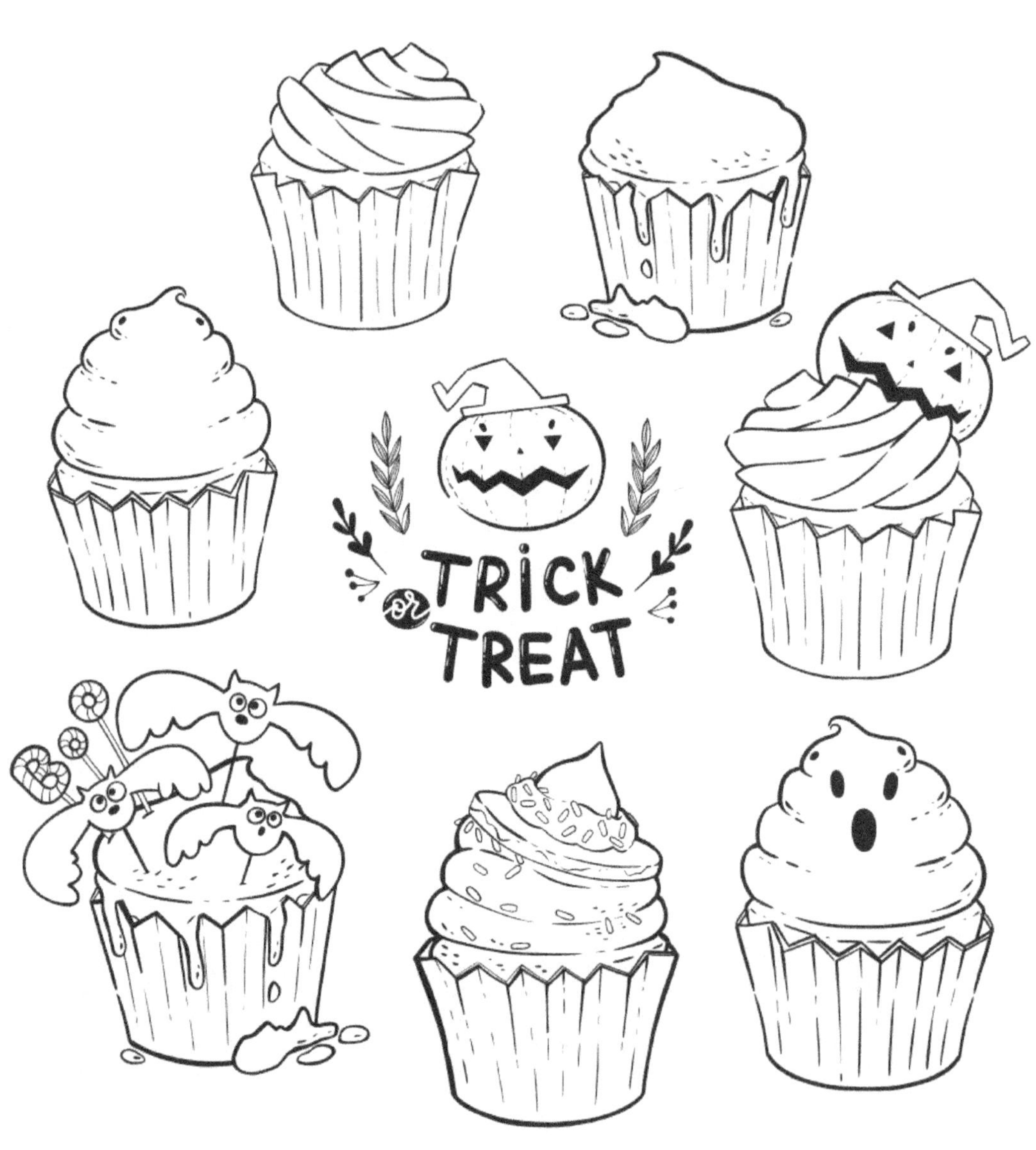

TRICK
or
TREAT

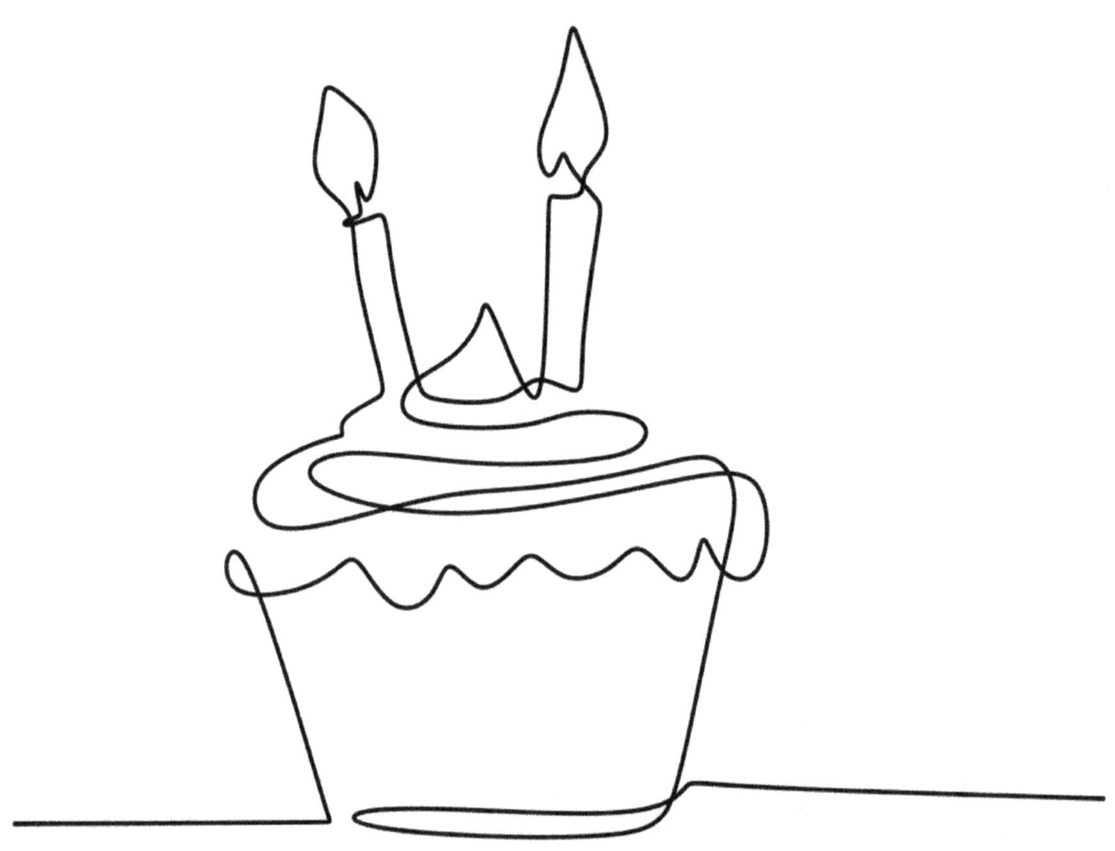

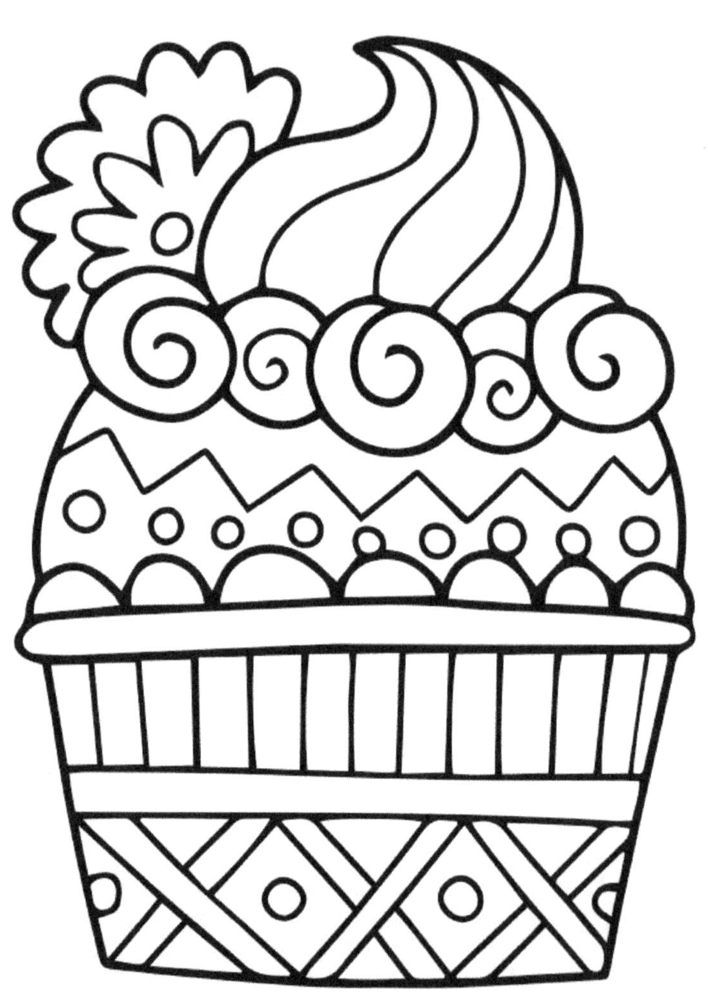

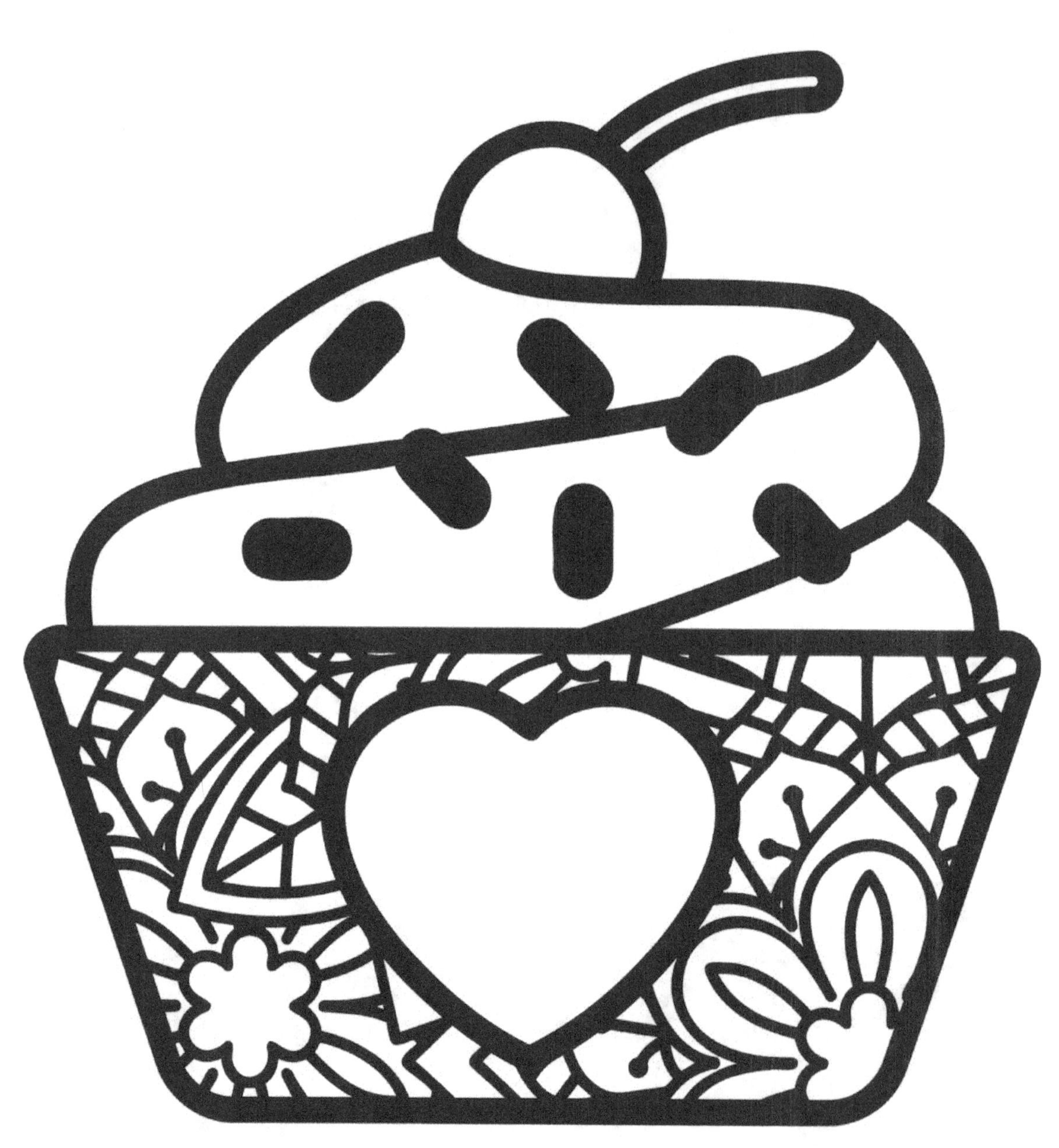

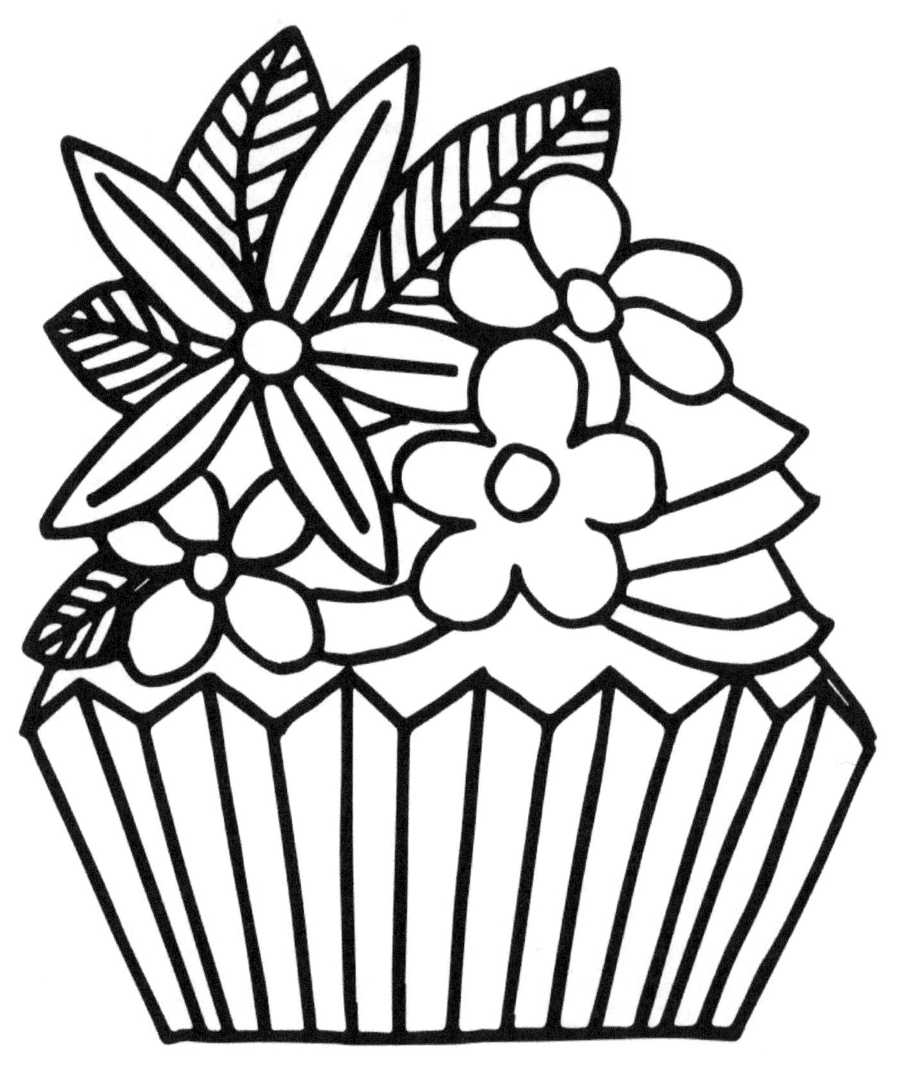

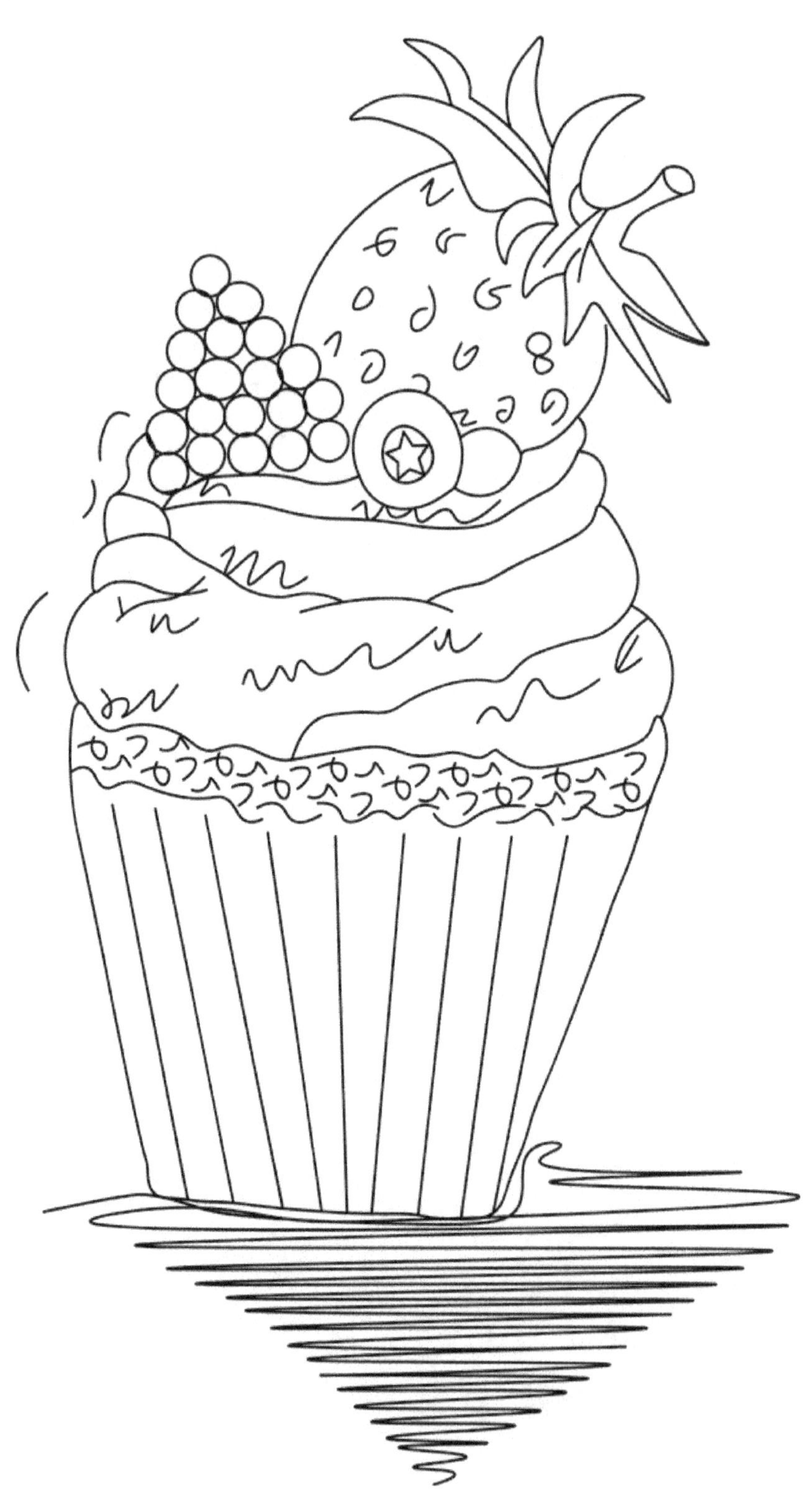

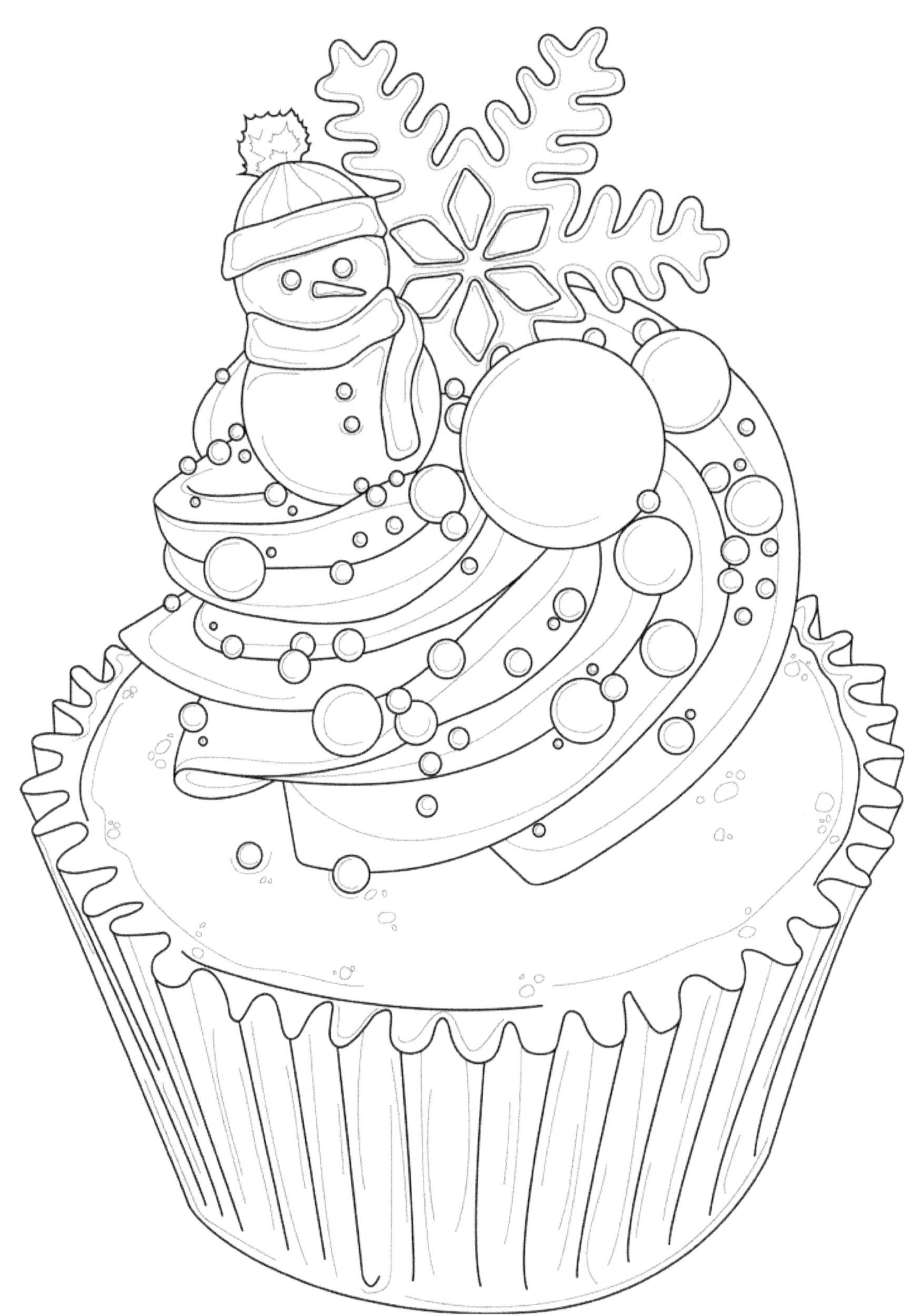

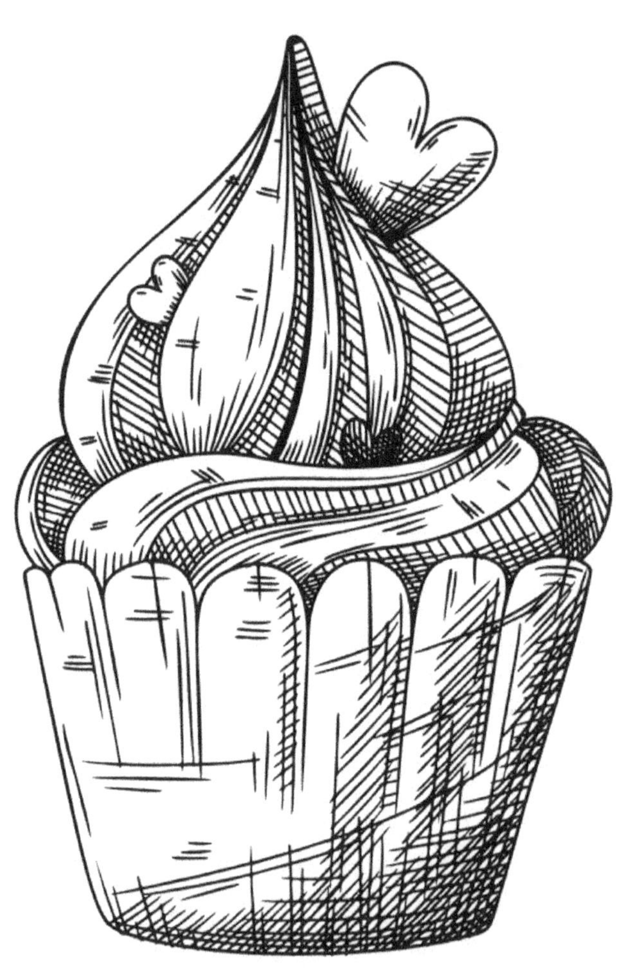

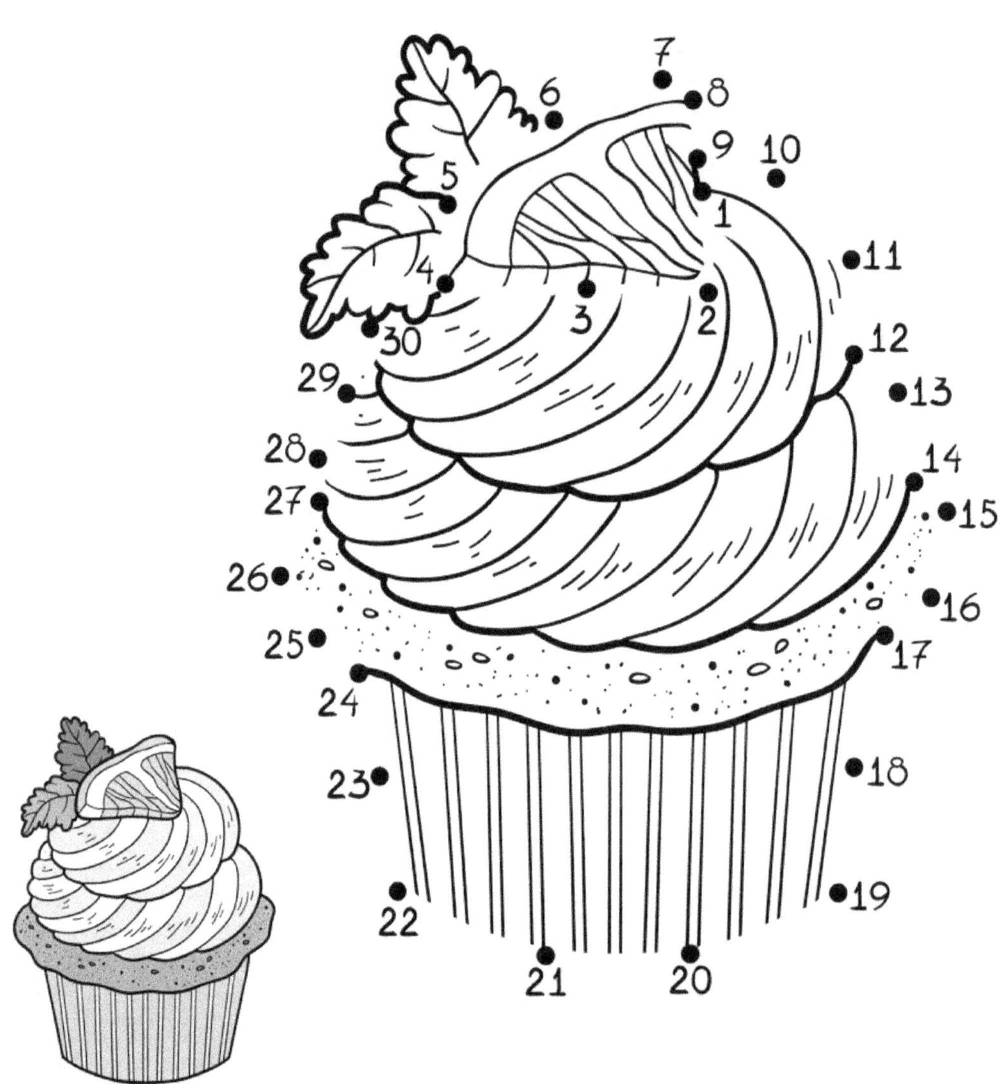

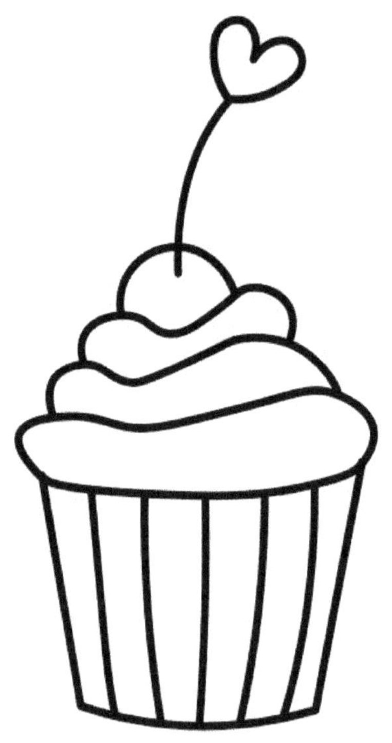

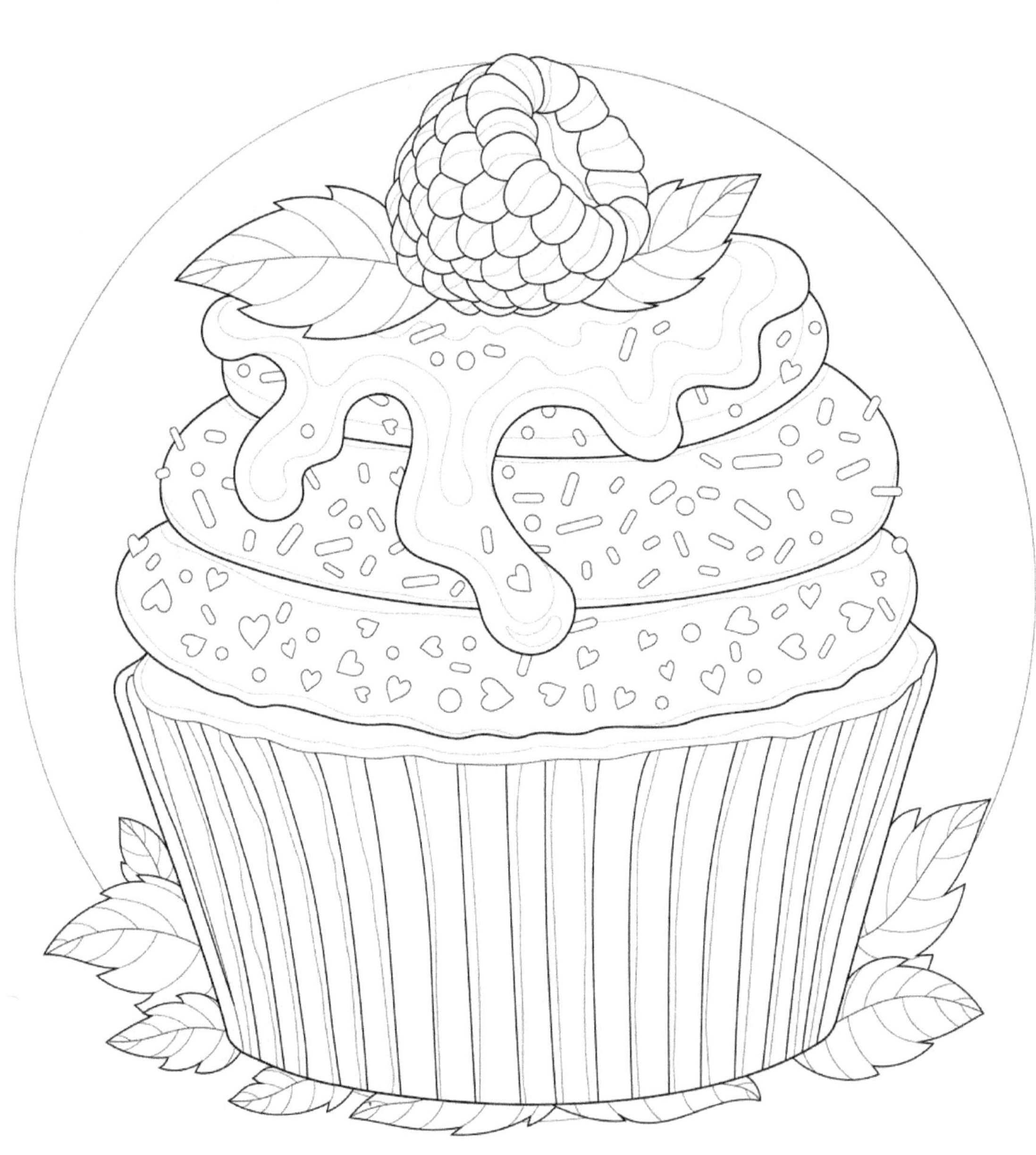

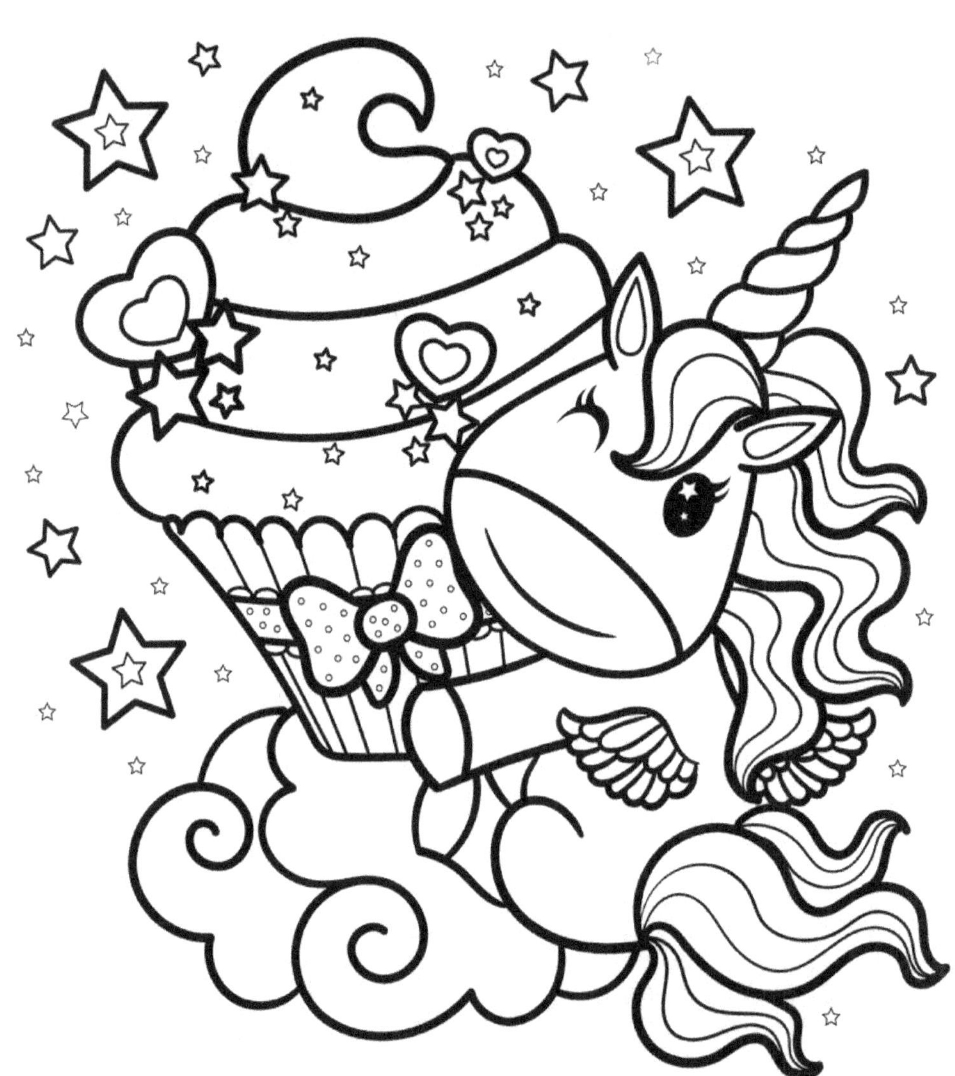

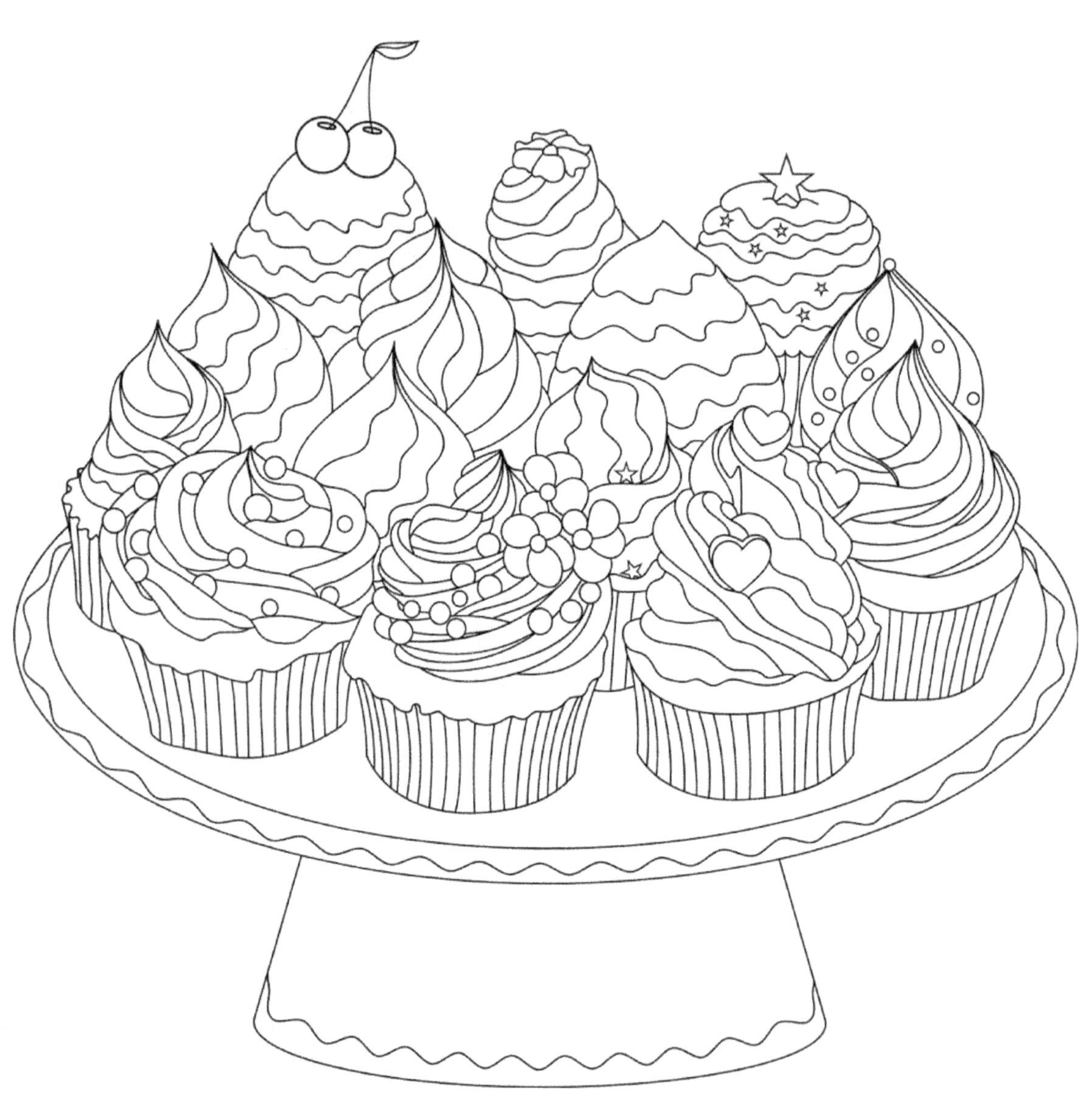

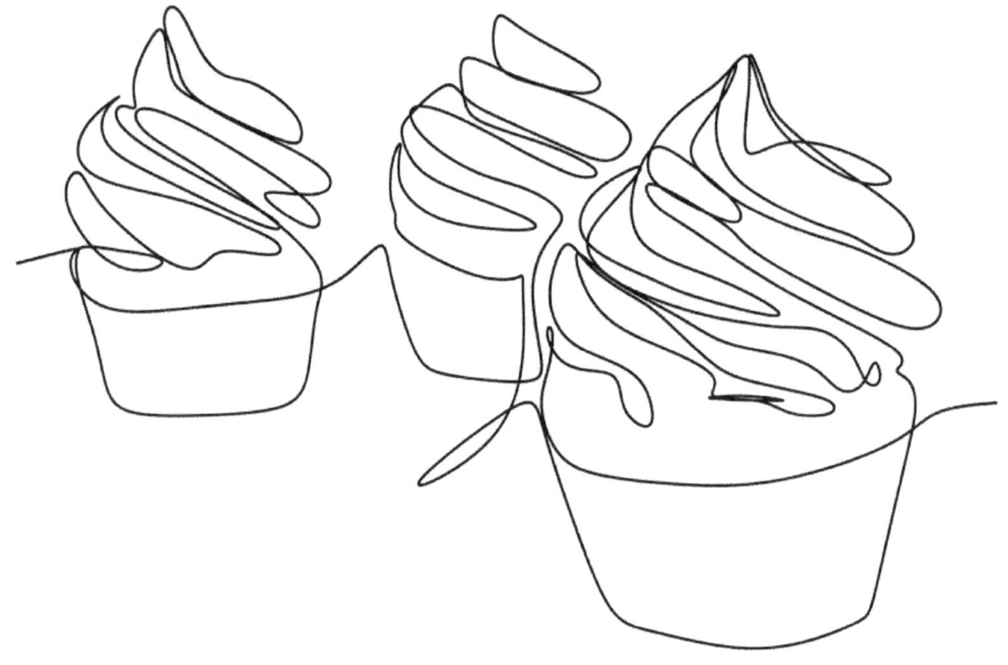

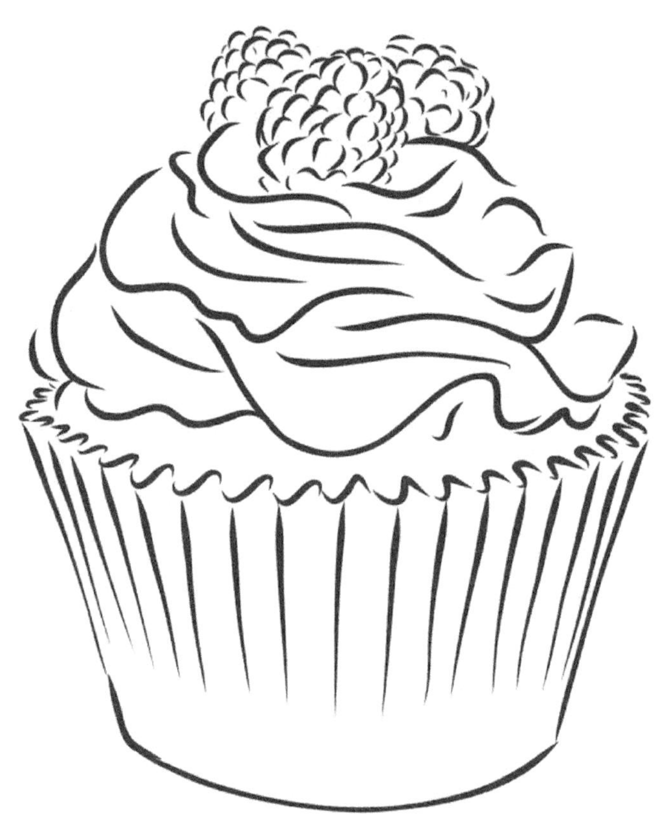

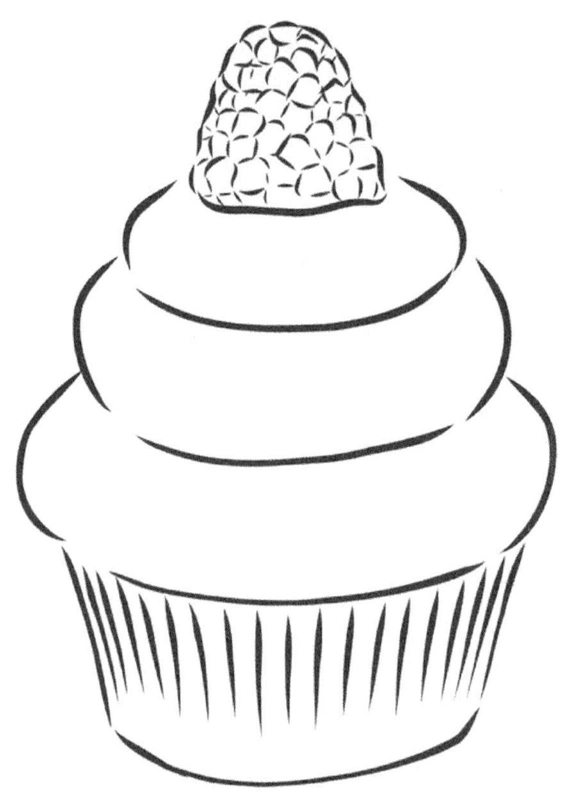

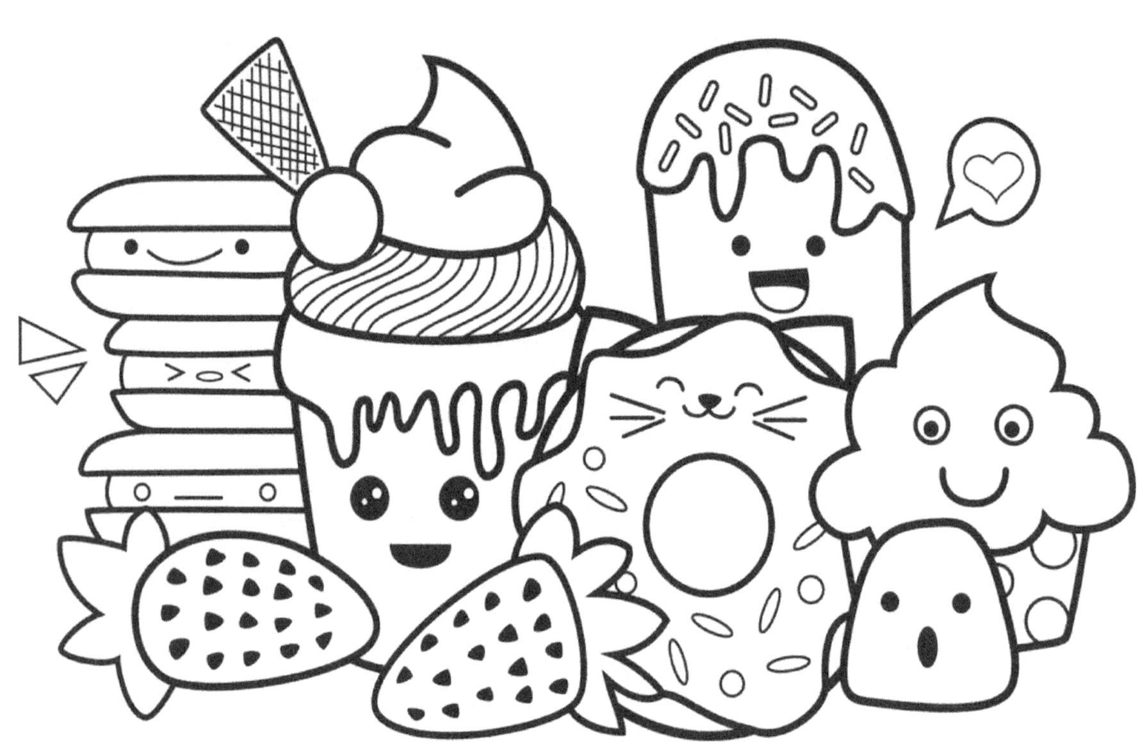

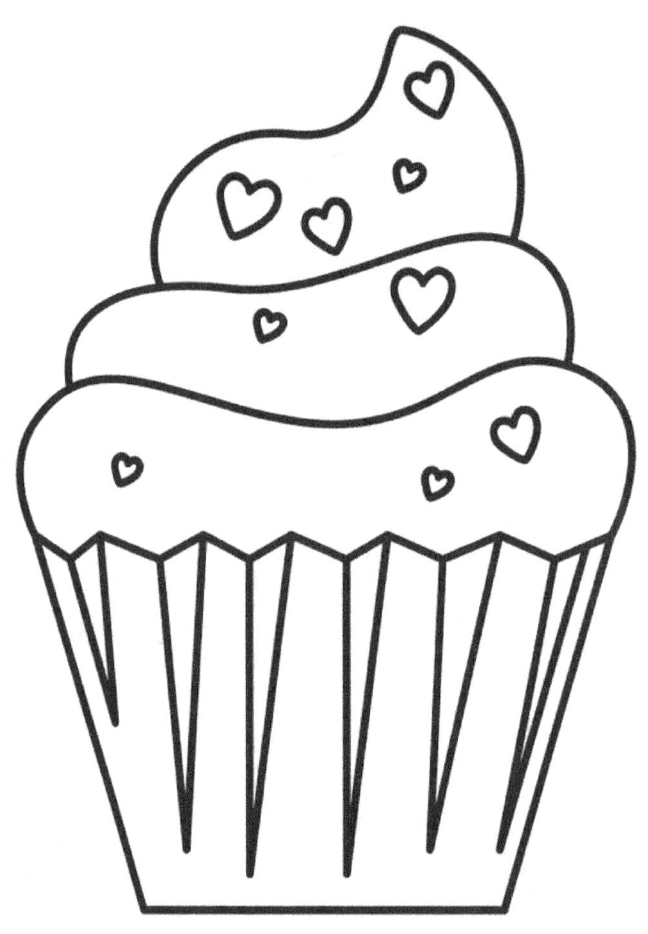

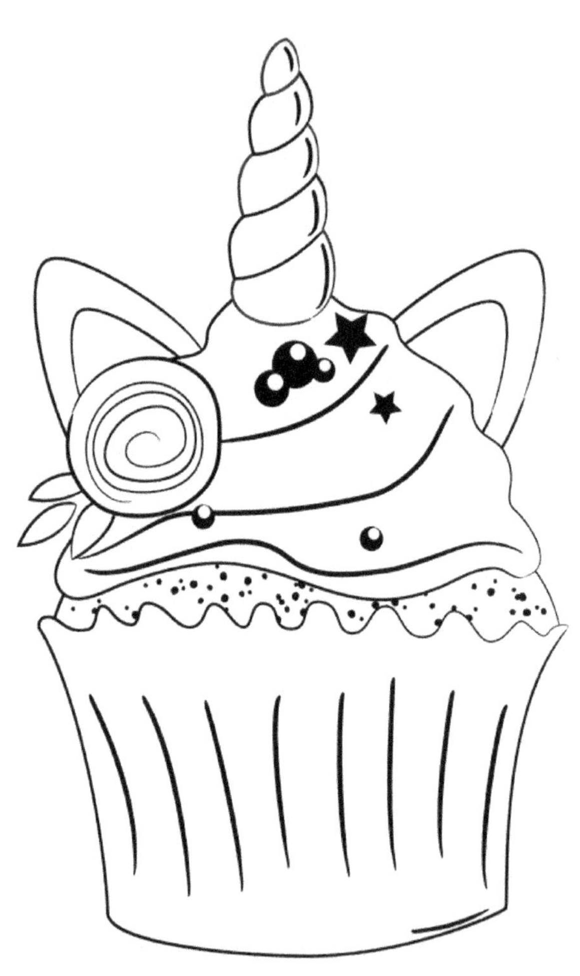

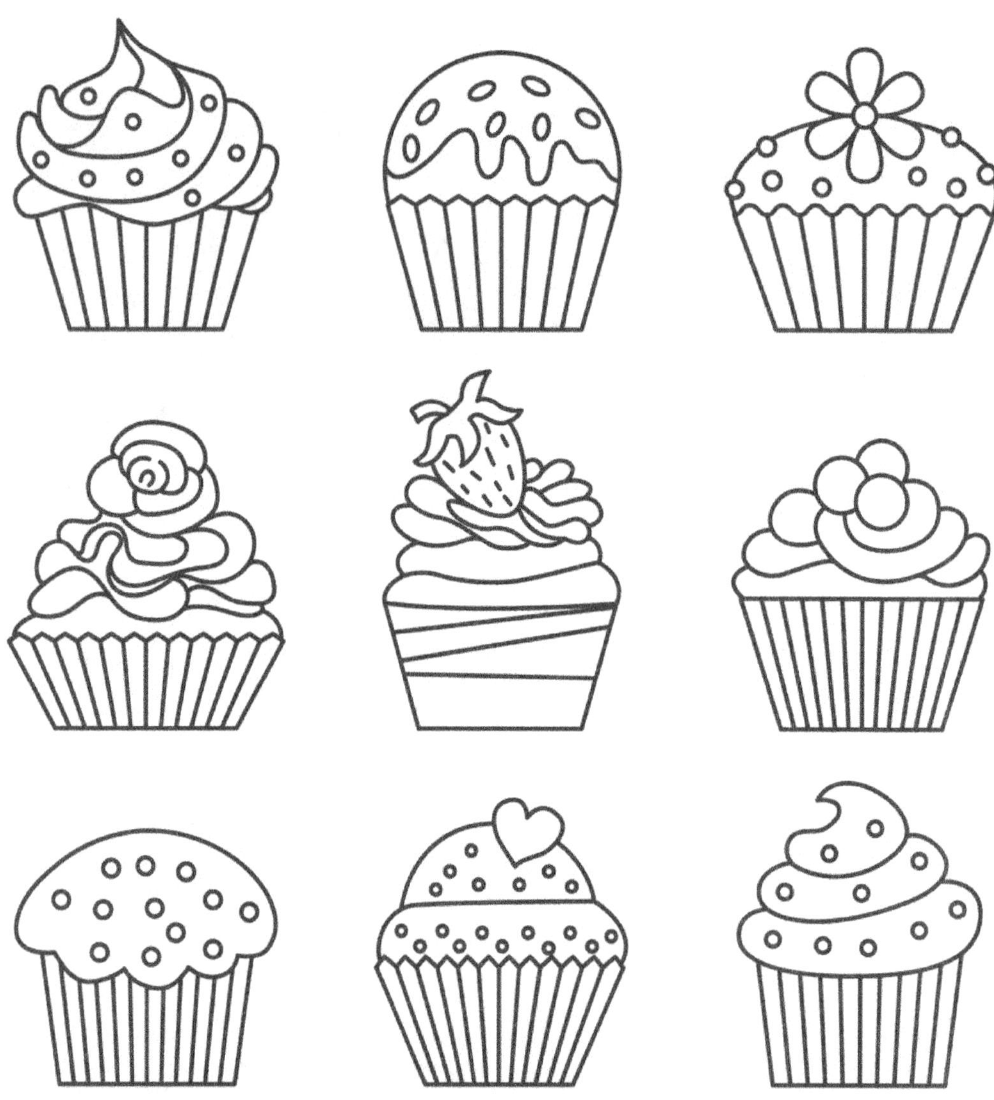

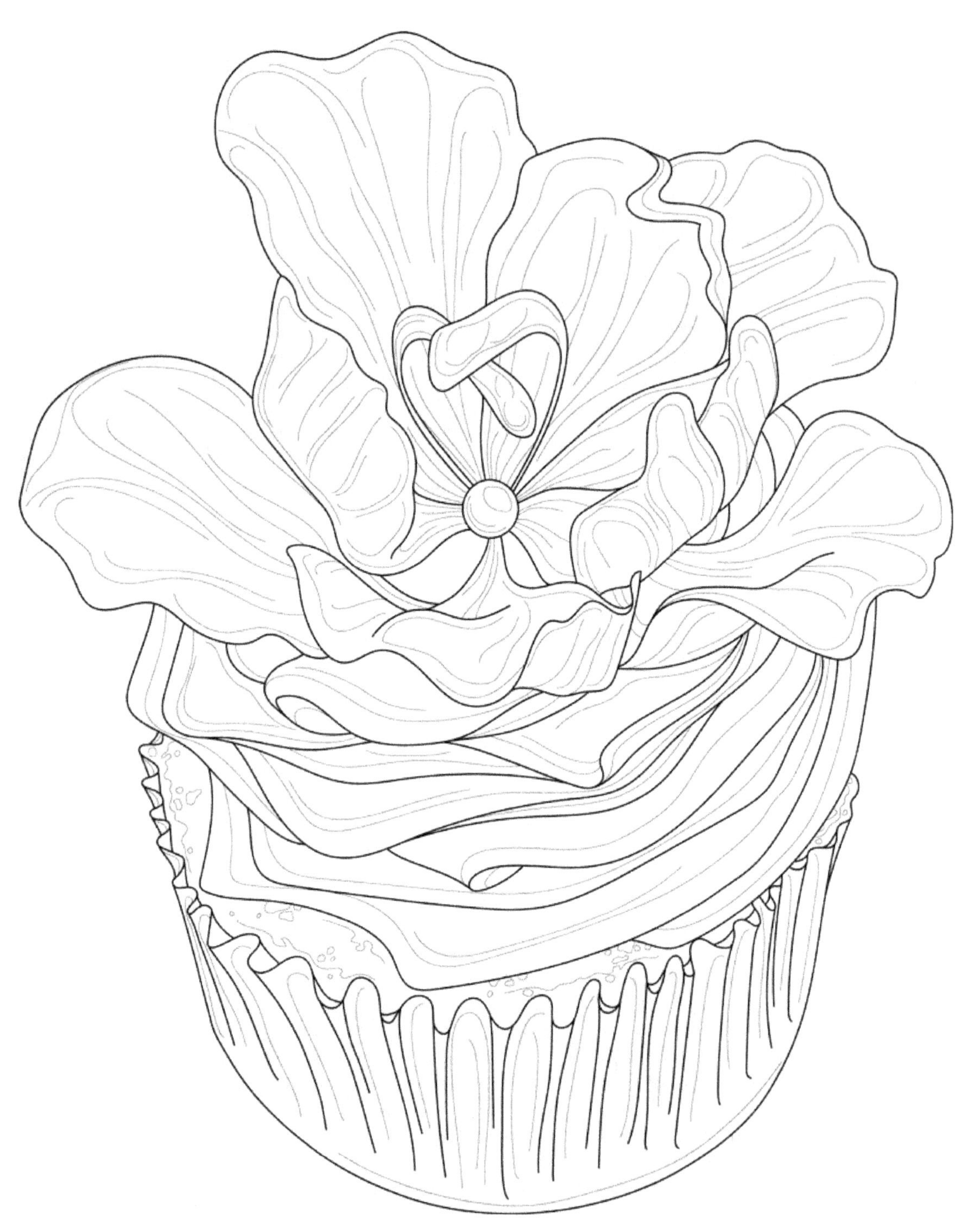

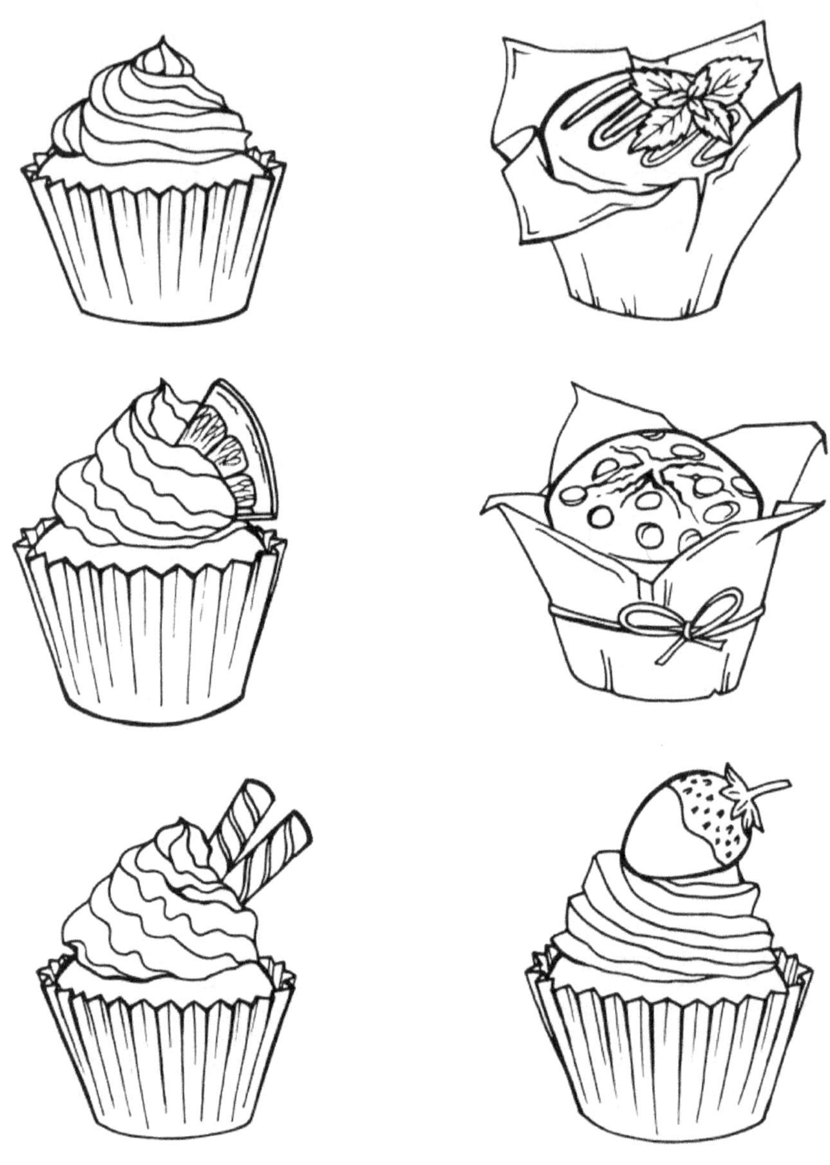

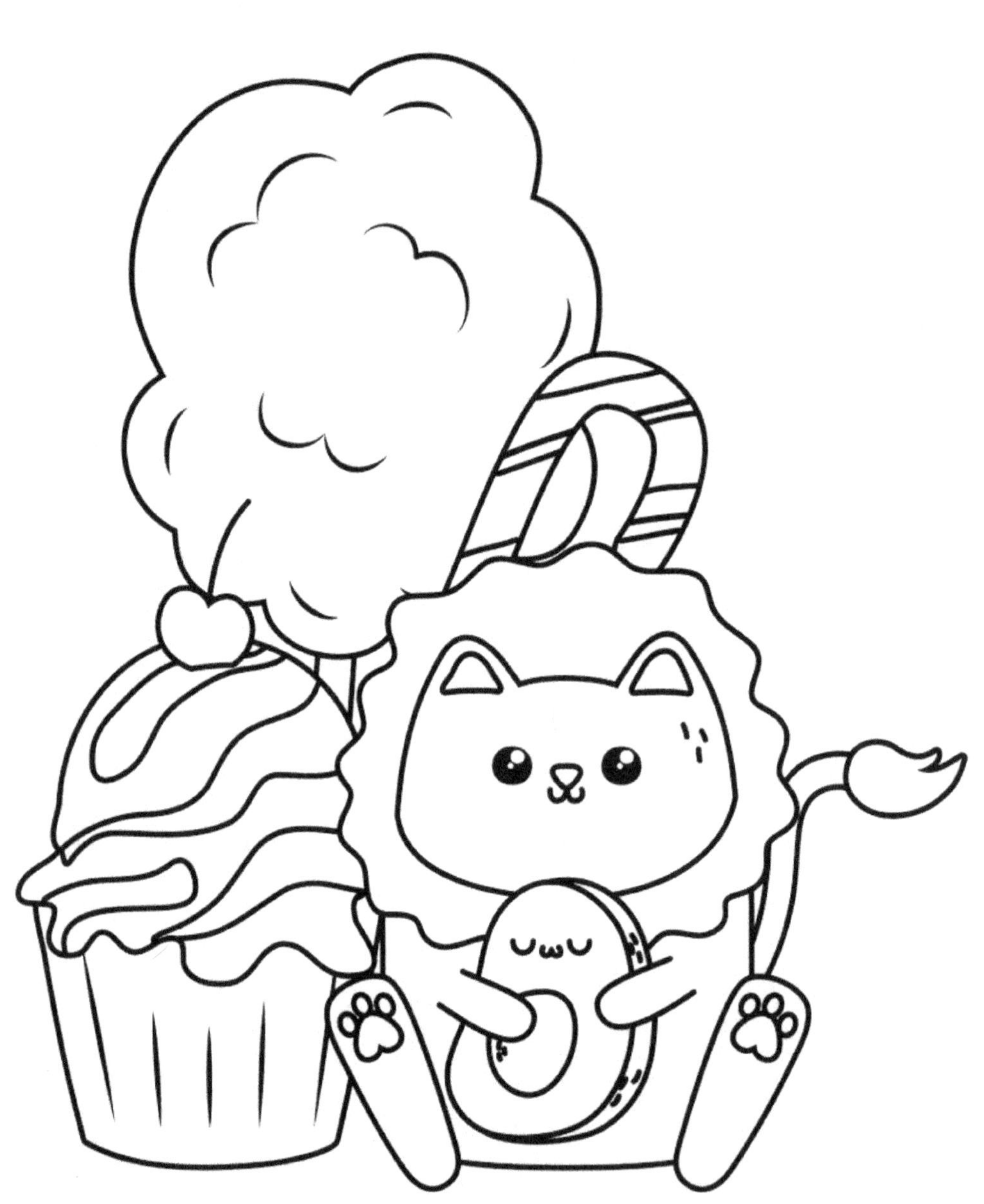

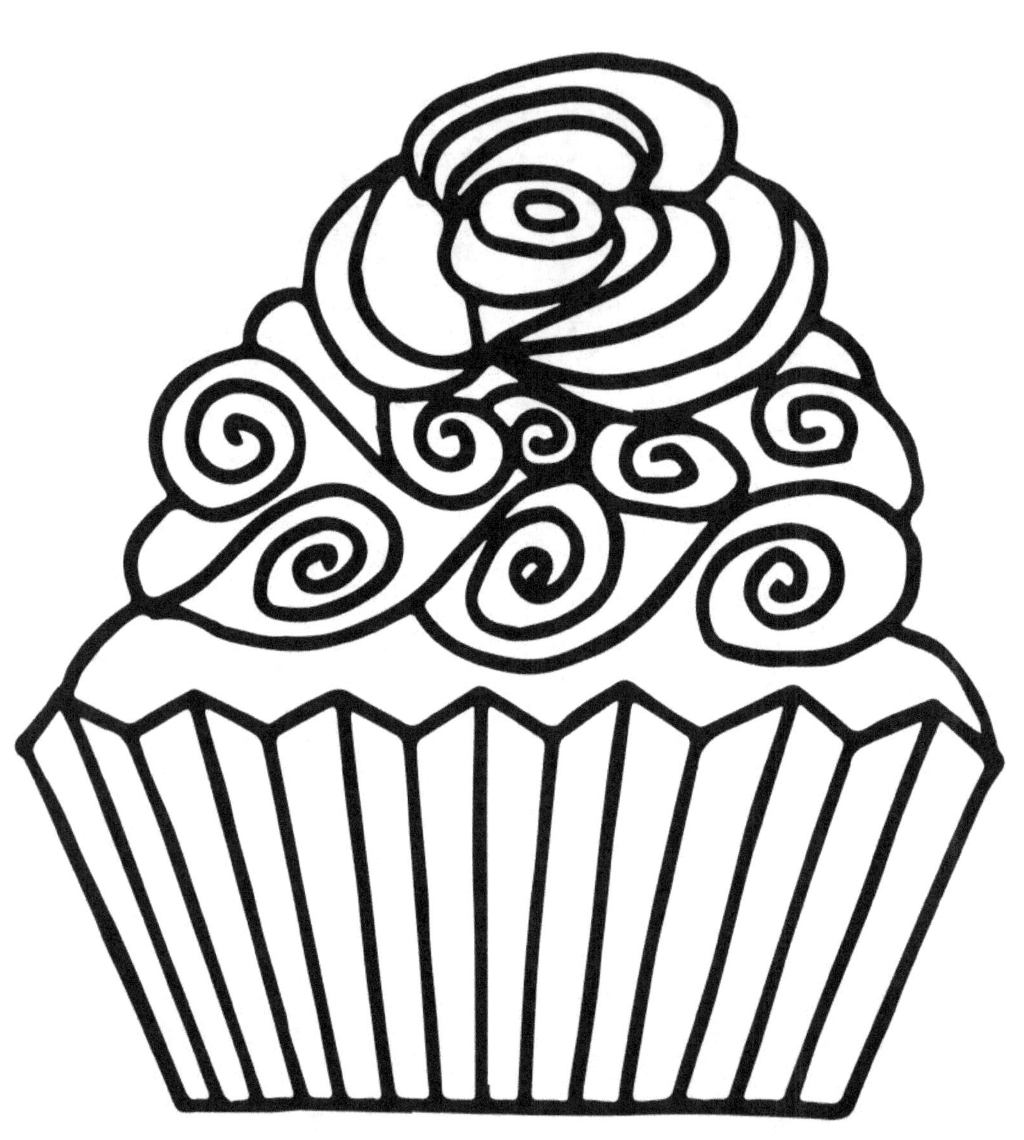

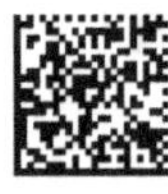